"Rich with stories from her own growth and the success of her clients, *From Type A to Type Me* provides a powerful step-by-step program to gain the essential habits—for stepping into a life with room for service and joy."
—Rikk Hansen, founder of Brilliant NEXT

"This book is a must-read for anyone who is serious about getting the most out of their lives, and who is ready to see things don't have to be done the hard way."
—Tara Truax, author of *Who the Hell Am I to Start a Business*

"[Melissa Heisler] shares powerful coaching techniques . . . to gain awareness of . . . how to find your path to living a life of purpose, acceptance, and joy."
—Regina Essel, author of *Embrace Today* and *Power Up Your Life*

"In *From Type A to Type ME*, Melissa Heisler . . . shares her story and the tools that helped her heal emotionally as well as physically, making her an everyday hero whose social change is rooted in gratitude. I am a big fan of this book, and Melissa [Heisler]."
—Joie Gharrity, founder of No. 113 Branding

For readers' reviews visit
http://www.amazon.com/From-Type-Me-Doing-Living/product-reviews/1940014417

From
Type A
to
Type Me

HOW TO STOP "DOING" LIFE

AND START LIVING IT

MELISSA HEISLER

For all those who supported and guided my journey.

ISBN 13: 978-1-940014-41-8

Library of Congress Catalog Number: 2014951008
Printed in the United States of America
First Printing: 2014
18 17 16 15 14   5 4 3 2 1

Cover design by Jessie Sayward Bright.
Interior design by Gabe Levine.
Illustrations by Melissa Amling.

Wise Ink Creative Publishing
222 2nd St. N, Ste. 220
Minneapolis, Minnesota 55401
www.wiseinkpub.com

CONTENTS

Preface ...... *ix*

Chapter 1: The Good, Bad, and Ugly of Type A 1
How to Spot a Type A......2
I Don't Have a Problem. Type A's Rule!......5
Take Control of Your Life—In a Different Way......9
Living with a Type A......11

Chapter 2: The Type-Me Alternative......14
Unique to You......16
Experiencing Not Doing......18
You Have the Power......22
The Magic Pill......25
Lessons Learned......31

Chapter 3: You Can't Change What You Can't See......32
The State of Gray......34
Finding the True Cause......42
Pull Yourself Back Together......46
What Are You Thinking?......52
Your Body Is Speaking to You......55
A Healthy Dose of Soul Food......58
Client's Type-Me Story: There Are No Coincidences......60
Lessons Learned......65

Daily Habit Options......66
The State of Gray......66
Association Awareness Query......67
Word Choice Query......68
Take Your Own Advice......68
Body Talk......69
Food Journal......69

Chapter 4: Release the Baggage......71
Reality Is Relative......72
There Are Absolutely No Absolutes......76
It's Not Me, It's You......80
Your Unique Type Me......82
Perfectly Imperfect......87
Just Say No......89
An Even Exchange......91
The Gift of Acceptance......94
Client's Type-Me Story: Me Is Singular......95
Lessons Learned......98
Daily Habit Options......98
Twenty Questions......98
Here Comes the Judge......100
Self-Talk......101

Chapter 5: We Always Have Options......102
The Infinite Peaceful Gray......104
Choose Your Own Experience......110
Sifting Through Your Filter......112
Write Your Story......118
Reprogram......124
Client's Type-Me Story: Taking Care of Me......129
Lessons Learned......133

Daily Habit Options......133
Expectations......133
Caught in the Act......135
Releasing Misperception......137
Prove It......138
Creating a Gray Scale......138

Chapter 6: Walk the Talk......140
A Constant State of Panic......141
The Power of GIA......146
Being Type Me......152
Habit Forming......158
Reacting to Constant Change......160
The Spiral of Life......161
Client's Type-Me Story: It Is . . . and Always Was My Choice......165
Lessons Learned......169
Daily Habit Options......170
Gratitude List......170
Gratitude Jar......170
Random Appreciation......171
Intentions......171
Pause......173

Chapter 7: Take Back Your Life......175
Timing Is Everything......176
Recovering Type A......178
Make It Real......179

Epilogue: My Journey from Type A to Type Me......181
A 3,000-Mile Journey Inward......183
Healing......189
Release and Recharge......196

Back to Reality......203
Uncovering the Type-Me Habits......205

Endnotes......208
Appendix: Resources......209
Books......209
Video......210
Studies......210
Acknowledgments......211
About the Author......213

PREFACE

When people tell me I have a peaceful aura, I can't help but smile. Having a peaceful aura is the last thing people would have said to me in the past. Most of my life I was a stressed-out Type A taking care of everyone and everything around me. At times I found enjoyment, purpose, and accomplishment by multitasking and completing projects efficiently and effectively. Other times I felt stressed out, overwhelmed, exhausted, and drained.

Over the years, stress, worry, anxiety, and all of the other side effects of being a Type A took a toll on me both mentally and physically. Not realizing stress was causing my physical pain, I searched high and low to find relief. After Western medicine, Oriental medicine, and alternative practitioners could not release my symptoms, I ended up in Peru working with a shaman.

In working with the shaman, I learned it was safe and beneficial for me to let go of unnecessary responsibilities and obligations. More significantly I learned I was creating my pain. It took thirty days of food and exercise preparation and ten days working with a shaman to relieve my health issues, but I am more powerful than regiment or healer. Heading home, after only a matter of moments in the Miami airport, all of the symptoms rushed back. I learned I am in control of how I feel mentally and physically, and most importantly, how I can change what I experience.

You can read the full story of my fascinating time in Peru at the end of this book. For now, let's explore how you can transform those negative aspects of a Type A personality, releasing you from the hamster wheel of stress to reveal good health, mental clarity, and joy in life.

CHAPTER 1

The Good, Bad, and Ugly of Type A

Being in control of your life and having realistic expectations about your day-to-day challenges are the keys to stress management, which is perhaps the most important ingredient to living a happy, healthy, and rewarding life.
— Marilu Henner, actress, producer, and author

You seem to have it all together. You appear confident, accomplished, and successful. You receive great reviews at your job. Your co-workers compliment your work. Your house is immaculate. Your children are expertly shuffled between school and practice. You are involved in multiple charities and organizations. Your friends wonder, "How does she do it all?"

But this story has another side. Your massage therapist regularly has to work on the stress and tension in your shoulders. Your doctor warns you about your blood pressure. Your personal trainer notices how, no matter the effort, those last few pounds don't come off. Your spouse is walking on eggshells due to your short fuse.

You don't see the warning signs. You think everyone has stress and tension. You know how to handle it. Besides, you have so much to get done, and *you* need to do it. Yet, if you are like I used to be, you also have constant tiredness, mild depression, and weariness, and require countless cups of coffee just to keep going. I would never tell anybody how badly I felt because according to everyone else, I was on top of the world. I was an amazing multitasking Type A. The truth is, millions of people are like you. The world sees them as competent and successful, yet they feel exhausted, and perhaps even empty inside. Trying to keep up with all of the work, stress, and struggle takes a toll. They can no longer sustain their busy lifestyle and are looking for a better way to do it all. Many people struggle with work-life balance as more and more of their time and effort is focused on their jobs. They are exhausted, but feel guilty or scared to let go of any of their responsibilities. Many Type A's hit bottom with their health, relationships, or work.

Being a Type A can be amazing, with the thrill of accomplishment and the joy of keeping everything in working order. Being able to plan, execute, multitask, and meet deadlines is awesome. The challenge is to use your Type A skills to your advantage, while not letting them control you. Things turn sour when Type A skills become rulers enslaving you, keeping you from enjoying life.

HOW TO SPOT A TYPE A

The concept of a Type A personality has not been around for long. It was identified in the 1950s by two cardiologists, Drs. Meyer Friedman and Ray Rosenman, who were studying coronary heart disease. They found a link between personality types and heart disease. According to their research, they identified three types of behaviors:

• Type A, which they labeled as competitive, ambitious, impatient, aggressive, and fast-talking;
• Type B, which is more relaxed and non-competitive; and
• Type C, which is hardworking, but becomes apathetic when faced with stress.

Those considered Type A were more prone to having high blood pressure, coronary heart disease, and stress-related illnesses.[1]

According to the Friedman and Rosenman study, Type A's are defined as:

- Having an intense sustained determination to achieve one's personal goals.
- Competing constantly against others and themselves in all situations.
- Having a persistent desire for recognition and advancement.
- Involved in multiple stressful activities tied to deadlines.
- Showing a tendency to rush to finish activities.
- Exhibiting mental and physical alertness over a long period of time.
- Practicing perfectionism.
- Taking everything too seriously.
- Unable to easily and clearly express their feelings.

According to Dava Money of the Creative Healing Institute, 50 percent of the United States population is now considered a Type A personality.[2] This is because the Type A personality is a learned, rather than an innate behavior. Our Western society rewards competition, success, focus on work, and being constructive. Additionally, modern technology provides new ways and new reasons to multitask and always be connected. The result is the desire and belief one must be a superhuman handling everything thrown his or her way. Because of this, most of us, at one time or another, experience Type-A tendencies.

Positive attributes of a Type A personality are being highly effective at work and home, having the ability to plan and meet deadlines proficiently, and handling multiple projects efficiently. Those with the Type A personality are also known to be dedicated friends. These are all wonderful traits. What I would like to draw attention to are the negative tendencies and results of being a Type A person. Type A's, and others caught up in our hectic world, may experience:

• Anxiety when we have to wait.

• Stress when our to-do lists no longer calm us down, but become our tyrannical masters.

• Being frantic, overwhelmed, and inexact due to a sense of heightened urgency.

• Being crazed due to clutter in the house and office.

• Feeling powerless to say no to responsibilities even when we become buried in them.

• Anger from others when we interrupt them because they are talking too slowly.

• Insomnia due to uncompleted to-do lists and unread email.

• Exhaustion from unrealistic multitasking.

• Devaluation as our focus on work means we are underpaid for the long hours we work and for what we deliver.

• Work-life imbalance keeping us away from the joy of family and friends, as well as our own needs and self-care.

• Martyrdom from an extreme desire to serve and give to others.

• Frustration by not being able to affect the emotions, actions, and results of others for which we feel responsible.

• Experiencing the emotions of others as if they were our own.

• Conditional love based on achievements or other self-created requirements.

When the behaviors of a Type A are out of control, we can take responsibility for situations and outcomes, for the feelings and experiences of others, and for absolutely everything around us. We think everything is our responsibility, and thus, within our control to affect. We fear if we don't take care of everything needing to get done, there will be horrible consequences.

The stress coming from being overtaken by our Type-A tendencies, eventually takes a toll on our mood, mental clarity, relationships, work satisfaction, and our health. The goal of this book is to help reduce these negative side effects of being a Type A before they cause major damage in your life, or if you have hit bottom, these tools can help you regroup and regain your life.

I DON'T HAVE A PROBLEM. TYPE A'S RULE!

Type A's rule! It is true. We are so efficient. We get so much done. We are so accurate. We are responsible. We are dedicated. We are hard working. We can do so much more, faster, better, and more accurately than those around us. We are so proud of all we can do. More people should be like us, right?

I have four important questions for you. Why are you a Type A? Why are you reluctant to stop being Type A? Who are you without the badge of Type A? What is the cost?

Why are you a Type A?

The Type-A personality is a learned behavior, so where did you pick it up? For many of us, it is because we are forced to become adults at a young age. We were given responsibilities, which as a child were way above our years.

Here are some ways we become Type A that you might recognize in your life:

• We came home to an empty house and had the responsibility for our dinner, homework, and household chores as our single parent was at work.

• We had an ill parent or a younger sibling for whom we cared.

• We were the youngest of many children, depriving us of early nurturing as we were forgotten or treated at the same maturity level as our older siblings.

• We were shown love for our achievements, so we pushed aside childhood pleasures to pursue accomplishments.

• We had an alcoholic or addicted parent, requiring us to step up into the parental role.

• We were in an abusive or otherwise unstable household where we learned to keep the peace by ensuring everything ran smoothly.

Whatever the reason, we learned if we controlled everything, then we were kept safe, we felt loved, and we knew we would be okay.

Why are you reluctant to stop being Type A?

The pride we have in all we accomplish, and all of which we are capable, is the usual reason we give for wanting to remain a Type A. The deeper truth is removing our Type A badge of honor is terrifying. Being Type A gives us purpose, gives our life meaning, keeps us, and those we love safe, and keeps the world spinning on its axis.

We fear if we release our Type A tendencies and don't take care of everything:

• Someone will get hurt, possibly us.

• We will become a destitute and homeless slacker.

• Things will fall through the cracks and the results will be devastating.

- We will be unloved and attacked for our mistakes.
- We will lose our jobs, finances, friends, family, and everything we hold dear.
- The world as we know it will stop functioning.

Who are you without the badge of Type A?

Do you have hobbies? Do you have passions? Or have you lost who you are to all of the things you are doing outside of yourself? If you took on adult responsibilities as a child, there was no time for you to be a child. You lost out on the time needed to explore who you are, and what you love. Without Type-A accomplishments and accolades, we have no self-worth and meaning. We don't know who we are outside being a Type A, and are afraid we will not exist without it.

What is the cost?

These are all significant questions to consider:

- Do you sleep well at night?
- Are you fit? Do you feel good in your body?
- What is your blood pressure?
- How is your digestion?
- Do you have close, loving relationships, or are those around you cowering after you gave your last order?
- Do you feel a slave to the needs of those around you?
- Do you celebrate your successes, or do you jump into the next task?
- Do you feel overwhelmed by all you need to do?
- Do you have work-life balance?
- When was the last time you laughed?
- How often do you smile during the day?
- How much do you enjoy what you are doing?

- How much of your day, life, and relationships do you miss because you are focused on the project at hand?
- How much of your life have you forgotten in a blur of completed tasks?
- Are you truly living your life or are you a machine frantically completing one task after another?
- Do you feel stuck, constricted, strained, and restricted?

The stress caused by letting our Type A behaviors command us is not a normal or necessary part of life. Unchecked, Type A-ism can lead to unhappiness, stress, dissatisfaction, and disillusionment. The desire to help others, an intense sense of responsibility, and the needs of loved ones take over our lives. Type A's can become consumed by responsibilities: obligations to family, requirements of work, responsibilities of a caretaker, and a never-ending to-do list. We begin to forget our personal desires and goals in life, and slowly lose joy, power, and even our identity. We become victims to the stress of work, the needs of others, a family history of dysfunction, and the fear of an ever-changing world.

I saw how these factors affected my experience of life. How the stress of a deadline or annual review wreaked havoc on my mental clarity, physical health, and my ability to be a true partner in my relationship.

If we can begin to see the negative effects of Type-A habits, we often feel powerless and terrified to change the way we act. We are afraid of losing control. We are afraid of losing our ability to function. Don't wait for the stress and strain of the Type-A lifestyle to have damaging effects on your health, relationships, and work. You can be in control a different way, and still enjoy the life you lead.

TAKE CONTROL OF YOUR LIFE—IN A DIFFERENT WAY

• You can feel you are in control and contributing to the world without having lists and deadlines rule your life.

• You can complete everything needing to be done, but in a way that is much better for your physical health and your enjoyment of life.

• You can enjoy life instead of feeling you are flying through it task by task.

• You can experience and enjoy accomplishments without having to burn yourself out.

As you adapt the Type-Me Habits, you will begin to see yourself as less of a victim, and more of a conscious chooser of your experience.

• You will find a way to fulfill your obligations, *and* still have time for yourself.

• You will be able to maintain a sense of self *while* still being a caretaker.

• You will be able to receive what you desire *without* guilt or justification.

• You will be able to remain powerful, calm, and energized, even in the face of incredible challenges.

Becoming Type Me does not mean you lose all the wonderful skills, tools, and abilities we Type A's have. It simply means releasing those behaviors not working for us, causing us stress, and damaging relationships. Becoming Type Me means gaining more of life. You gain the space to find more time, more joy, and more ease with your projects. Type Me reduces stress, allowing for better health mentally and physically. As a Type Me personality, you will gain more joy in your relationships, and in all you do.

The Type-Me Framework shows you a new way to approach

life. Instead of trying to control every situation and everyone around you, you can learn to control how you experience what is happening around you. Think about your life. Have you really been able to control others or situations? If you did, was the experience joyful and free, or was it filled with constraint, frustration, and discomfort? True freedom from stress lies in changing how you approach life.

In Peru, I felt for the first time what it was like to be completely free of any worry or restraint. It was a feeling much deeper than just the normal holiday getaway. When we are on vacation, we usually experience some joy because we are outside of our normal routine. On vacation, we have no household chores, bills to pay, or bosses breathing down our necks. My experience in Peru took things even deeper. Those around me did not judge me. I had no feelings of personal worthlessness. I experienced no Type A habit of constantly watching the clock and adhering to a schedule. I felt no nagging resentments from the past, or fears of what would happen next. Instead, I had an indescribable sense of calm-centered joy. Type-Me Habits recreate this stress-free, pain-free joy every day in every situation, all without the help of a shaman or medicinal cactus as experienced in Peru. The practical, no-nonsense Type-Me Habits help you to feel safe, fulfilled, healthy, calm, relaxed, self-assured, decisive, clear-minded, flexible, and joyful.

Type-Me Habits:

• Are down to earth and relatable, making them easy to implement into your life.

• Are frank, honest, and practical, providing a clear understanding of why and how you can make immediate changes to your life.

• Were developed by a recovering Type A, so they are pragmatic, concise, efficient, and effective.

• Guide you to take responsibility for your experience.

Instead of trying to change others or circumstances, you learn the power of adjusting your focus, perceptions, and judgments to control how you experience and live. Through Type-Me Habits, you will improve your mental and physical health, increase mental clarity, more easily deal with difficult people, and find peace in your current work situation. It is time to get back into the driver's seat of your life. Embracing Type-Me Habits will provide you with true power and control over your life.

LIVING WITH A TYPE A

Whether it is your spouse, sibling, loved one, employee, co-worker, or boss, we all have a Type A in our life. Type A's can be snippy, demanding, dominating, frantic, harried, nitpicky, obsessive, party poopers, uncompassionate, non-stop, and robotic. But in the end we love them—or we are forced to work with them.

The most important aspect of a Type A is they are really scared, although they appear to be confident and in control. Type A's use tasks, projects, and lists to feel secure. They are obsessed with perfectionism and getting things done because they think it makes them safe. The ability to relax and enjoy life terrifies Type A's because it feels dangerous when so much needs to get done, or they feel unworthy of receiving.

Keeping these few things in mind will make dealing with the Type A's in our lives easier.

• Provide a framework. Type A's are lost without their list, and without knowledge of what to expect. Have a clear plan or set of expectations.

- Provide a clean space. Maybe it is not possible to have a clutter-free house or office, so designate an area to be clutter free. This can calm them down.
- Walk away. Their drama is not your drama.
- Know their triggers. Certain people and situations will take them blindly into manic Type A mode. Be prepared.
- Acknowledge their contribution, even if it is provided in a brisk or adverse manner. Type A's live to give, and feel resentful when their giving goes unrecognized.
- Type A's can be demanding, but it is never about the task they want completed. Find out and resolve the true pain they are trying to appease with the task.
- Protect yourself by taking control of the controller. Don't let them take responsibility for what is important to you, or what you want to handle yourself.
- Have compassion. Even though Type A's can be controlling, know they are as tough or tougher with themselves.

If the Type A in your life has accepted the challenge to transform from Type A to Type Me, there is a powerful way to help them: create a code word. When I was consciously trying to transition, I wasn't always aware of when I was falling into my Type-A ways. I gave my husband a code word to say when he saw me being Type A. Using the code word took me out of the knee-jerk mode, and made me aware of my actions. Use the word sparingly, or it loses its power. Using a code word takes a lot of trust on both sides. The Type A must trust he or she will just be reminded, not judged. The helper must trust he or she will not be attacked when drawing attention to the Type A's actions. Be sure both parties are committed before agreeing to work together.

If you use a code word or any of the suggestions above, remember not to take responsibility for changing the Type A in your life. Changing is their responsibility. You can guide and suggest, but when it comes down to it, the Type A has to be ready and willing to change. While they are making their transition, support them but also remember to take care of yourself. Don't let their transition negatively affect your mood or your life.

The tools outlined in this book will give you insight into how Type A's think and more ideas on how to make your relationship with them better. Plus, Type-Me Habits are also powerful tools for the stress we all feel in our lives. One of my clients, Tom, is not a Type A. He is a very even-keeled man who goes with the flow. However, when I met Tom, he was exhibiting the negative symptoms of Type A because of a demanding job. He was rushing, making mistakes, felt he couldn't say no to assignments, and was not sleeping or caring for himself. Hopefully, like they did for Tom, these tools will be able to provide you with some relief from your day-to-day challenges as well.

CHAPTER 2

The Type-Me Alternative

*When I was five years old, my mother told me that happiness
was the key to life. When I went to school, they asked me what
I wanted to be when I grew up. I wrote down "happy." They
told me I didn't understand the assignment, and I told them they
didn't understand life.*

— John Lennon, musician and singer-songwriter

An alternative to the negative effects of the Type A personality,
and the stress we encounter in our lives, is to be a "Type Me."
Awareness, Acceptance, Alternatives, and Actions are the four
habits necessary to become Type Me. Focusing on these habits
provides you with a new way to live your life with less stress, and
more control. I will go through each habit briefly here; however,
I devoted a whole chapter to each habit so you can truly understand each, and how to use them to improve your life.

• **Awareness** is often the first habit I introduce to clients.
We spend so much of our lives reacting, and so little of it truly
understanding what we are experiencing. Awareness is where
we become a non-judgmental anthropologist, uncovering
our feelings, beliefs, thoughts, actions, and reactions. For us
recovering Type A's, this can be a difficult habit because we

have nothing to "do." The Awareness habit is not about fixing, changing, creating, or removing anything. The function of the Awareness habit is to reacquaint us with an objective eye to ourselves, warts and all. This habit is important because without self-awareness, no changes can be made.

• The **Acceptance** habit is where we work through our perceptions, beliefs, and judgments of ourselves and others. The goal of this habit is to accept the truth of the situation, not the story we are telling ourselves based on our bias. This is a powerful habit because it releases the stress of perception. This is where we can begin to let go of our victim status, and feel the power of being in the truth of the situation. It is also an important habit because if we cannot see the truth of the situation, we cannot change the situation, or our experience of it.

• The habit of **Alternatives** is when we empower ourselves by releasing the constraints of black-and-white thinking. Often we are stifled by what we perceive are our only options. We believe we either have to accept the pain we are in (black), or we choose something that is usually perceived as worse, impossible, or unattainable (white). When we are stuck in black-and-white thinking, it is difficult to uncover the myriad of other choices available to us in the "gray." The Alternative habit helps us use our new perceptions to create and act upon new options.

• The final habit of **Action** helps us through our life's journey. Focusing on what we have, instead of what we don't, keeps us in the present moment. Throughout our lives, we will be challenged. Maintaining our own unique Daily Habits is the foundation of a less-stressful life. No habit will continuously impact your life, unless you practice it consistently. Understanding this material is not enough to change your life. True change comes from *living* a new way of being.

The habits are not necessarily sequential. The order I present them in this book is the order I often introduce them to my clients, but not always. These habits are not linear. You may need one habit more than another at different points of your day or week, depending on what life throws at you. You may already be excelling at one habit, so focusing on a new habit may be important to you. No one habit is more important than another. No hard-fast sequence is followed. As you will learn, this program is an outline of tools, not an absolute procedure. Releasing absolute rules and expectations is the foundation of being a Type Me, and so the Type-Me Habits should be seen as flexible tools and guidelines, not commands.

UNIQUE TO YOU

The habits presented are just guidelines. The habits you adopt should be unique to you. Type-Me Habits are simply a framework. How you execute these habits in your life may look different. Think of each habit as a building block, but you determine what is in the building block. No habit is one size fits all. Meditation works for me, but my husband can find the same place of peace when he is washing his boat. Neither way is better or "right." The only right is what is right for you individually.

The Type-Me Habits are about self-discovery, self-worth, self-respect, and self-empowerment. They are not about following my system, or becoming what I tell you to be. When I asked my clients for their stories about how these habits have helped them, I was amazed at the range of how these building blocks affected their personal and business lives. We each have our own challenges, stressors, and perspectives. Use the framework of the habits to affect what is most important to you right now, and in the way that works for you.

Some of my clients have a hard time with this. Gail is what I call a seeker. She is always trying the newest exercise craze, diet, or spiritual practice. Gail constantly looks for the new guru or practice, and then she adopts it as her own. As we started exploring the habits together, she had a hard time creating her own habits. She wanted to know what I was doing, and would emulate me. For Gail to grow into herself, she had to create her own. She had to take responsibility for her own life, and how she led it. As I encouraged her to try new and different habits until she found the right ones, Gail released herself, and uncovered who she truly was.

Type-Me Habits are about empowering you to be *you*. You are not taking on a system outside of yourself. It is a process to help you find the answers already within you. Type-Me Habits are a framework to help you step into your own unique power. The habits are simply guides to help you empower yourself.

This book will provide you with the framework, but the habits are your sandbox to play in. Explore what works for you, and throw out the rest. If you have ever tried to diet, you know how hard it is to stick to a menu if you don't like how the food tastes. Make these habits palatable to you. I would rather have you practice your version of the habits, instead of pushing yourself to conform to my personal Daily Habits—and either be frustrated or quit.

Create your personal Daily Habits by what feels good to you. Absolute right and wrong don't exist. Some things will work for you, and some won't. Consider it okay. Create your habits from your center, your heart, and your core. Do not follow my personal process—unless it resonates with you. Ensure your habits are in alignment with you.

Feel free to create and adapt your habits at your own pace. Some things may come easily. Others may not. During your journey, grow into your habits bit by bit. Every day strive to make your life just a little bit better. Take your time building your habits. Just like strengthening any muscle, ease into it, and work at it every day.

EXPERIENCING NOT DOING

The first shift to make in order to embrace Type-Me Habits is adjusting how we define joy. Most Type A's define joy based on accomplishments, titles, awards, meeting deadlines, material possessions, professional success, societal approval, and following traditions. However, many times the pressure to achieve these goals creates pain instead of joy. The problem is not with choosing the wrong versus right things. The problem is in believing "things" provide us with joy. Things don't provide us with joy; it is *experiencing* the thing that brings us joy. The Type Me definition of joy is in what we experience.

Joy is an experience. Joy is experiencing life fully in the present. Joy can be experienced through things, but joy is not inherent in the thing itself. This is apparent if you have ever seen a child enjoy the box the toy came in as much as the toy itself. Joy is truly experiencing all the inherent physical and emotional aspects of life. The joy I experienced in Peru had nothing to do with the sites we visited, or the gifts I purchased. The joy was from the experience of finally being in touch with me. The joy was from actually *feeling* and being in each and every moment. True joy is not found in clicking off our checklist, but in deeply experiencing the act of doing and accomplishing each item on the checklist.

We are redefining what living life to the fullest is all about.

Living is a verb, not a noun. Joy is found in *living* our life, not just having a *life*. Life is about the experience. When we give a child a toy, they find joy in experiencing the toy. There is no inherent joy in the toy itself. Joy is found in our interaction with life. Joy is found in the act of living.

Much of the pain we feel is wrapped up in things, the nouns. Nouns are deadlines, expectations, and outcomes, which are usually outside of our control. The desire to control what we cannot causes pain. When the physical outcome is different than what we desire, it can lead to self-attack, depression, and disappointment. When we are anxiously waiting for a thing, we often miss out on the experience happening in the moment. When we tie joy to something outside of ourself, we cannot truly feel joy.

Things are transitory. Our experience is truth and eternal. No one can take away or steal what I feel, or what I experience. We usually try to change the nouns in our lives to make us happy. We want a new job, a new house, or a new spouse. To truly change our lives, we need to change the verbs in our lives. We need to change how we *experience* our job, house, and spouse.

Henry was recently divorced, in a difficult financial situation, and overweight. He believed if he had a million dollars, all his problems would be solved. I could see how his desire for this money, this noun, was an obstacle to his happiness. Henry believed he needed this money to be happy. We talked about what he wanted to do with the million dollars if he received it. Henry wanted to buy a new house, travel, and pay off his bills. He could hire a personal trainer, and he could have the freedom to spend more time with family and friends. I asked how he would *feel* in the new house. How does he *feel* when he travels? How would he *feel* if all his bills were paid? His answers were connected, invigorated, and secure. Instead of working on manifesting the money (noun), we spent his sessions working on having these feelings (verb) in his life, right now. Henry didn't need the house to feel connected; he just needed to be more conscious when he was with his family. He didn't need to travel to feel invigorated; he could experience each day as a grand adventure. Henry didn't need a hefty bank account to feel secure. No amount of money can *create* the feeling; he had to *choose* the feeling. When we finished working together, Henry's pain was gone, and he had a new lease on life, all without one more dollar in his pocket.

As a recovering Type A, I always hated the saying, "It is not the destination. It is the journey." Type A's are all about the destination. We are focused on finishing tasks, projects, and assignments. Because of our focus on a future outcome, we often miss most of life because we are not in the present moment. In uncovering the Type-Me Habits, I finally came to understand this adage. I always looked at the first half of the axiom, the "it is not the destination" part. I felt without a destination or a goal, life was meaningless. I also thought the phrase meant taking pride in reaching our goals was wrong or bad in some way. I was completely missing the power of the second half of the phrase. Focusing on the journey releases us from the pain of outcome. It does not matter if the outcome is bad or good. Focusing on the future, or a result, takes us away from enjoying the moment. Focusing on the journey means we do not miss any part of life. Focusing on the journey means we are aware and alive in each moment. Focusing on the journey means we are living our lives, not just having a life. Focusing on the journey is focusing on our *experience* of life's journey.

Joy is found in what we experience (verb), not what we have or achieve (noun). If we have been playing the victim for a long time, we may say we cannot have joy because we are at the mercy of circumstances and the actions of others. Since we cannot control these things, we cannot experience joy. What we can control is how we *experience* those circumstances and actions. The truth is we *choose* our experience. We may not choose what happens to us, but we can choose how we perceive and experience what is happening to us. We are not victims of others or outside circumstances. Our power is from within. Our power is in our ability to choose and create our own experiences.

South African Nelson Mandela was sentenced to prison. He spent eighteen years on Robben Island doing hard labor in a quarry, and another nine years at Pollsmoor Prison. He was only allowed one visitor a year and one letter every six months. The prison guards were told to be rough with Mandela. By all appearances, this was certainly a situation where one could justifiably feel like a victim. Mandela knew he had a choice. He knew he could create his experiences. He chose to embrace and treat his guards fairly, even if they did not reciprocate. Mandela felt he would lose himself if he lost his love for his fellow man. The result: often the warden had to replace Mandela's guards because, once they experienced his kindness, the guards could not be severe with Mandela.

We each hold the power to make our life better. When we look to others, things, or the latest quick fix, we give away our power. By accepting the fact and responsibility for controlling our own experiences, we are empowered. Reducing our stress starts with a willingness to make a change, a willingness to use your inherent power. It is a commitment to uncovering and adhering to your own Type-Me Habits. It is not a commitment to outcome. It is a commitment to developing and accepting a new moment-by-moment lifestyle based on your personal Type-Me Habits. It is a commitment to being self-empowered.

YOU HAVE THE POWER

The final shift to embrace Type-Me Habits is accepting the power you have to change your experience. You are the only one who can affect the life you lead. Releasing the responsibility and blame placed on individuals, events, and circumstances empowers you to see what is truly in your power. Sometimes we are afraid of our power. In *Return to Love: Reflections on the Principles of "A Course in Miracles,"* Marianne Williamson said, "Our deepest fear is not that we are inadequate. Our deepest fear is that we are powerful beyond measure. It is our light, not our darkness that most frightens us." It takes courage to step into our power. Many of us were not taught or encouraged to use our power. Women especially are consciously and unconsciously taught to be good, quiet little ladies. We are taught to be in the passenger seat. We are taught to follow rules and authority. Eleanor Roosevelt said, "No one can make you feel inferior without your permission." The truth is, we are empowering others through our submission. When we fully embrace our power, we become our own authority.

Sometimes we are not aware of the power we possess. If you have grown up in an atmosphere where we believe we are victims of circumstance, how could you realize and cultivate your power? Much of our Western culture puts us on a conveyor belt, pushing us through a cookie-cutter system. We go through grade after grade of school, learning the same curriculum in lock step. Individuality is discouraged. Uniformity and staying small is rewarded. We learn to feel safe by following rules, and completing assignments. This results in an inability to truly know ourselves, and learn what we are capable of doing. As you learn the Type Me framework, and apply it to your life, your unique personal power will soon be revealed to you.

Sometimes we feel we are powerless to change our life now, because of what has happened in the past. A dear client of mine,

Cynthia, tortured herself emotionally because of choices she made in her youth. As a teen, she became pregnant and gave up the child. Afterward, she was full of guilt and remorse. Cynthia thought she was broken and worthless because of her choice twenty years earlier. She kept herself from feeling and accepting joy because she believed she did not deserve it. She would not allow herself to feel good after what she had done. When we worked together, Cynthia came to accept her decision, and most importantly to leave it in the past. Cynthia could do absolutely nothing now to take back what happened. Punishing herself for her choice kept her stuck and unhappy. We changed her focus to the present. She could do nothing to change the past, but what she could do was to make the best choices today. Every day is a new day. She has the option in every moment to choose anew. Cynthia is not a victim of her past. And neither are you.

Accepting the power to change your life means admitting we cannot always change circumstances or the past, but we can change ourselves. It is within our control to change our thoughts, beliefs, perceptions, actions, and reactions. We create our experiences by choosing how we perceive circumstances and events around us. Nelson Mandela showed this glowingly. You may not be at the point to accomplish what he did, and you don't have to be right now. All you need to do is accept the premise.

Jeremy was diagnosed with an incurable, and at times, painful cancer. He spent the last five years of his life going back and forth to doctors, and in and out of the hospital. Yet through it all, Jeremy maintained a positive and happy attitude. A few months after he was diagnosed, his wife, Jill, was also diagnosed with cancer. Her cancer was found and removed through a routine procedure. Jill did not receive chemotherapy or any other post-operative treatment. Instead of gratitude for a quick-and-easy resolution, Jill lamented about her disease, creating a litany of "what if's" that never materialized. She obsessed over what would happen if her cancer returned and she couldn't care for Jeremy. She was angry about their misfortune. She tormented herself with fears, worries, and anxieties.

How much of their individual experience was based on the facts of their circumstance, and how much of their experience was within their control? Jeremy's circumstance of a painful and incurable cancer was certainly more difficult than Jill's procedure. However, Jill suffered more mentally than Jeremy by how she chose to experience her circumstance. If we understand we can change our experience through changing our thoughts, beliefs, perceptions, actions, and reactions, then the circumstances really do not matter. Neither Jeremy nor Jill could change their diagnosis. They could not change the circumstance. Yet Jeremy changed his experience without changing his illness. We cannot always affect the physical things in our lives (jobs, illness, relationships, living conditions, previous choices), but we can always make changes internally, and affect the experience of our lives.

Making internal, personal changes is the source of self-empowerment. Blaming circumstances creates victimization and stress. If you have trouble running a marathon, you cannot change the length of the race, but you can still improve your experience. You can choose to train every day to increase your stamina, you can choose to increase your strength by working with a trainer, you can purchase shoes that make your run easier, or you can focus on doing your best with every footstep, instead of being obsessed with how long it takes you. Life is a marathon. Stop blaming the difficulty and length of the run, and make choices to improve your experience.

THE MAGIC PILL

After Peru, I searched for a "Magic Pill," a quick fix allowing me to feel like I did during my time with the shaman. I will tell you a secret: the magic pill doesn't exist. Permanent relief is not found in a one-time thing to do, receive, or buy. The way to take back your life from stress is by changing how each and every moment is approached. Remember, *it is not the destination; it is the journey.* These habits are not a one-time event or process. To change your life, you need to do it continuously, moment by moment. It is the reason why these are Daily Habits. They are not something to learn, have your life changed by, and then move on. The key to making permanent changes in your life is by creating Daily Habits to help you through everyday stress. These habits also give you a solid foundation to manage when major stressful events occur.

After you have read this book or any book you find helpful, you may expect to be stress-free and happy forever. But being happy is like caring for your body. If you eat a healthy, balanced diet one day, but for the rest of your life you eat nothing but couch stuffings and fingernail clippings, will you be healthy? The same is true for your mental, spiritual, and emotional health. Changing your attitude, perception, and actions for one day is not enough. It is necessary to create and integrate new healthy habits, routines, and ways of life every day. The Type-Me Habits are a daily practice. The lessons I impart are not one-time learnings, but daily, moment-by-moment reminders of how one can live a better, less-stressful life.

We cannot solely rely on attending workshops and reading books to make lasting changes in our lives. We need to do the work: go through the exercises, be vigilant every day, and constantly exercise our new mental and emotional muscles to ensure these new learnings remain ingrained. If we don't, after we leave the workshop or close the book, we eventually lose all the knowledge and slide back into old habits.

After I returned from Peru, I noticed how easily the new lessons learned receded as my focus turned to my day-to-day responsibilities. My challenge and quest were to find ways to integrate this new way of being into my daily life. We are here to balance our lives—to hold down a job and take care of the family, while also taking care of ourselves. We shouldn't have to wait for our yearly vacation to find peace, calm, and happiness. The goal is to find joy every day while we are in the midst of the stressful real world in which we live. We are hit by pain, anger, fear, and stress every day. To keep this pain from piling up, the Type-Me Habits are a Daily Practice, a constant companion keeping us from being buried by the challenges of life.

In 2011, I had the honor to witness a panel discussion with the Dalai Lama and representatives from the three Abraham-tradition religions: Christianity, Judaism, and Islam. It was an amazing event of open-minded individuals who believed in their faith, but respected and understood the faiths of others. The discussion showed how the core lessons from these major religions were similar, and through embracing this knowledge, acceptance, compassion, and peace could result. *I was high as a kite.* I felt the love of the speakers, the love of the audience members, and even felt the joy of physically embracing a friend who I didn't know was going to be there. After the discussion, I walked down the streets of Chicago smiling at everyone I passed, seeing their inner good, and sending them peace and love. Next, I met my afternoon networking appointment. In the first ten seconds, the individual appeared to be self-absorbed, rude, and negative. My body shifted in my chair. I closed off from him verbally, physically, and energetically. I shut down. Then I laughed. Ten minutes after feeling enlightenment and fully conscious, all it took was a few words with this man to send me back into anger and the us-versus-them, black-and-white mentality. Great job, Melissa. I took a deep breath and consciously, actively shifted back. I looked at this man, and could see he was scared. I began to understand he appeared abrasive so he could feel safe. I sent him loving and accepting energy. And you know what? As I softened, he also softened. It wasn't enough to make us best friends, but it was enough to make a cup of coffee with him tolerable. The big lesson from this is the importance of staying vigilant every moment of every day. We are not perfect, and neither is anyone else we meet. We are going to be constantly challenged. If we want to find peace and happiness, we can't just learn these lessons and move on. We need to incorporate them into our daily lives.

My neighbor is a lovely man. He takes our recycling bins in when we are out of town, and he has helped us find contractors for house projects. On more than one occasion, I have also seen him helping out our other neighbors. He is a great guy with one unique obsession: his driveway. No matter what the season, he ensures his driveway is pristine. He blows grass off it in the summer and leaves off in the fall. In the winter, we see him outside every time a half-inch of snow accumulates. No matter the temperature, or how hard the snow is falling, he removes every flake. Most days his driveway is cleaner than my kitchen table.

A few winters ago, the Chicago suburbs were blessed with quite a heap of snow. Without fail, my neighbor was out there every hour or so constantly removing any trace of the white powder. He not only does his driveway, sidewalk, and steps, but he ensures every ounce of snow is removed from the street surrounding his drive, lest any white stuff makes it back onto his beloved concrete. In the days before I worked from home, I had to be out of the house early for the morning commute, allowing the snow to pile up on my driveway all day long until I got home.

At night, I would struggle to remove the two, three, or five inches of the snow, which accumulated while I was away. When I began working from home, I started to follow my neighbor's lead, and shoveled more frequently. What I learned was shoveling snow a few times a day means the amount of snow shoveled each time is smaller, making the weight of the snow lighter and easier to manage. Frequent shoveling also makes it easier to remove any ice patches forming due to tire treads or footprints. I found myself spending more time removing the snow, but the actual effort of removing it is much, much easier. Plus, I am able to remove all of the snow, reducing ice and other buildups.

Often we let our feelings of pain, frustration, stress, guilt, or anxiety grow and grow until they are overwhelming. When we can't take anymore, we finally get a massage, take medicine, get some counseling, go on a retreat . . . or take a mystical trip to Peru. Our efforts alleviate some of our pain, but they don't remove all of it. The amount of stress is just too much to go through. We let it pile up, and now it is too heavy and large to deal with in one sitting. Like trying to clear eight inches of snow after a long day at the office, the process is difficult and seems overwhelming. Each shovel full is heavy and hard to move, and we are left with patches too frozen and deep to remove. Instead, imagine if you spent a few minutes every day clearing away your anxiety, fear, stress, and frustration. Frequent clearings make it easier to remove any build-up, and keep stress levels low because they are never given a chance to build.

Here are a few points to remember and use for your own Type-Me practice:

• **Don't let it pile up**. Work at it every day. Don't wait until you have a nervous breakdown or a major medical issue to force you to examine your life. Address issues as they occur.

• **Small loads make easy work.** Working on things a little bit at a time makes it easier. Instead of having a major issue to deal with, work on things when they are small. They take less time and are easier to dispel. Waiting until they grow larger makes it harder to remove them. Try to address small issues in the moment they arise, before they grow into something bigger.

• **Be consistent.** Even when things are terrific, take the time to examine what is going on. A little insignificant annoyance today could become something greater over time. Remove it before it has time to grow and fester. Take the time every day to examine your mental state, even if you are feeling blissful.

A benefit of staying on top of your emotional, physical, and mental wellbeing is you also feel much better. Shoveling away the anxiety every day will keep you from hitting rock bottom. Each day will be better because no issues linger from the day before. You will be starting from a clean slate. If your mind and emotions are clean at the beginning of the day, it becomes much easier to spot potential issues as they stand out in contrast to the rest of your peaceful wellbeing.

To keep my area clear of stress, I have created my own personal Type-Me Daily Habits.

My Awareness Habits

• Every morning spend at least fifteen minutes in the "State of Gray." I will repeat this time again in the afternoon if I am feeling stressed, confused, angry, or depressed.

• Take a walk or do yoga to wake up and get connected to my body.

• Take breaks as needed to keep stress levels from rising.

• Be constantly aware of my thoughts, words, and actions.

• Be aware of any times I feel constricted, and consciously uncover their source.

My Acceptance Habits

• Every morning, read from an inspirational work to gain insight into Acceptance of self, others, and reality.

• Use Twenty Questions to help identify the truth in every situation.

• Be aware of and release judgments which arise due to my perception, versus the truth of the situation.

My Alternatives Habits

• When I feel stuck in an unsatisfactory situation, identify and choose the best alternative from all those available.

• At the end of the day, see what could have been handled differently and if any issues are yet to be resolved.

My Action Habits

• Think of five things to be grateful for before getting out of bed.

• In the morning, write my gratitude, intentions, and affirmations.

• Answer "Fantastic!" when someone asks how I am. This is a great way to remind myself how I want to be.

These habits are my way of staying connected to the power of Awareness, Acceptance, Alternatives, and Action. Please note these are my habits. Since we are all unique, so are our habits. As you work through the next chapters, start noticing what works for you. Choose some practices that resonate with you, and leave the others behind. Feel free to adapt any of these practices to your personality, abilities, needs, and beliefs. Add any practices you currently have. As you go through the chapters, practices, and tools in this book, it's very important you take the time to create your own Type Me Daily Habits. Reading this book will give you a pop of insight, but it *will not* make any changes in your life if you do not take action.

Hopefully, you now have a clearer idea of how Daily Habits of Awareness, Acceptance, Alternatives, and Action can reduce the stressful side of being Type A, and help you maneuver through major stressful events. In the next few chapters, you will learn more about each Type-Me Habits, and how to use them to empower you to have a joy-filled life.

LESSONS LEARNED
• The Type-Me Habits of Awareness, Acceptance, Alternatives, and Actions are your unique, customizable framework for power.

• Joy is found in the act of living, and being in the present moment.

• Each of us is responsible for and empowered to affect our lives for the better by changing our thoughts, beliefs, perceptions, actions, and reactions.

• The way to reduce stress and maintain a joy-filled life is by working at it each and every moment of every day.

CHAPTER 3

You Can't Change What You Can't See

*Let us not look back in anger or forward in fear,
but around in awareness.*
— James Thurber, cartoonist, author, journalist, and playwright

As Type A's we are naturally hyperaware, but this awareness is usually focused outside of ourselves. We are powerfully aware of everything external to us.

- We see what others are doing.
- We see situations to be fixed.
- We see potential problems to be addressed.
- We see circumstances and their effect.

We have limited visibility, however, of ourselves.

- We don't see how when we rush, we make mistakes.
- We don't see how our focus on negativity brings us down.
- We don't see how taking care of others keeps us from caring for ourselves.
- We don't notice how our stress is affecting our health.
- We don't see how the way we think, believe, and act is damaging our lives.

To make changes in our lives we need to shift our focus from external to inner awareness. True awareness is:

• Getting back in touch with, or maybe realizing for the first time, one's personal truth.

• Seeing what is really happening around us without the filters of perceptions, judgments, and expectations.

• Noting our actions, reactions, and words to realize the effect they have on our experience of life.

• Hearing the messages from our body when our mind can't get through to us.

• Being intuitive and having the "feeling," which is truth even when the mind disagrees.

• Using the power to shape our experience by our beliefs, thoughts, words, actions, and reactions.

• Understanding the interplay between our mind, body, and spirit.

In the world of computers, before new software is added, it is first necessary to identify and remove any old versions of the software or any other software which may interfere with what we want to install. The same goes for our lives. Before adding new healthy habits, it is first necessary to become aware of, identify, and remove any habits, beliefs, and constraints conflicting with the new goals. For example, we cannot improve our feeling of self-worth if we have a tape of the *one time* someone belittled us constantly playing. We need to identify and become aware of our current programming. We need to become aware of how we see the world, how we interpret others' actions, how we judge ourselves, and how we create the stories of our lives in order to make beneficial changes.

One must explore what thoughts or beliefs exist now that threaten the new desired input. It is identifying which of your current beliefs conflict with the beliefs and perceptions you would prefer to have. Also, it is being aware of how your body feels after eating certain foods, without certain foods, and with different amounts or types of exercise. It is tapping into your intuition or spirit to be aware of what "feels" right and what does not, what resonates with you and what repels you, what is part of your Type Me and what is not.

Awareness is where we put on our anthropologist hat. This is simply a time to research and uncover. It is *not* a time to make any judgments or conclusions. The power of Awareness is collecting the clues of what does and what doesn't work in our lives. If we jump to conclusions or rush to judgment, then we could lose important pieces of information. When we are in Awareness, it is very important to remain impartial to the information we collect from our mind, body, and spirit about our current state of being. We need to uncover and understand our unique Type Me and all the interrelated systems of us. Without this impartial Awareness, we cannot make appropriate changes. We must be aware of what exists now in our life before we can improve upon it.

THE STATE OF GRAY

The foundational tool to help you become more aware is what I call the State of Gray. The State of Gray is simple, and yet can be very difficult. Eckhart Tolle, author of *The Power of Now*, calls it being in the now.[3] Martha Beck, author and columnist for *O, the Oprah Magazine*, has called it doing nothing,[4] and most recently, wordlessness and oneness. Back around 500 BC, the philosopher Lao Tzu called it wei wu wei, or doing not-doing.[5] Don Miguel Ruiz, author of *The Four Agreements*, calls it refusing to obey the voice of knowledge.[6] Buddhists refer to it as mindfulness. I like to call it the State of Gray, a peaceful space between black-and-white thinking. No matter what this state is called, how it is described, or how one gets there, it is the very simple concept of turning off the mental monkey chatter of our left brain so we can truly be in the moment. Being in the State of Gray allows us to be free from thoughts of the past or future, free from judgments and expectations, and free to just be and experience.

Being in the State of Gray means existing in a singular moment without judgment or false perception. It is not labeling the black or white, the past or future, the good or bad, the beautiful or the ugly, the loved or hated. It is a state of pure existence without judgment. Our minds are constantly creating stories, making judgments, interpreting, and labeling. The State of Gray stops the stories—and allows us to experience the truth without the filters of our minds.

The State of Gray exists on its own. It is not affected by the past nor concerned with the future. Nothing in history is of relevance. The State of Gray is a fresh start. It is the truth of the moment without the tarnish of the past. Our minds like to bring along all of our baggage: every perceived stupid thing ever said, every misstep taken, every event we wish we could do over, every hurt experienced, every disappointment received. But none of those memories is the reality of the moment, and none exists in the State of Gray. The only thing absolutely known to be true is what is currently sensed and experienced without personal filters of perception and judgment. The State of Gray provides a *pure spot of truth* and is the gateway to our Type Me.

Being in the State of Gray allows the true experience of the act of living. Life is about daily moment-by-moment experiences. Many of us don't focus on these moments. Instead, we are focusing on our next meeting, vacation, purchase, or life achievement.

Don't get me wrong; it is important to have a goal for what is next. But all too often people who are so focused on what is next, can't enjoy what is right now. Many times we are tainting our current experience with negative expectations based on the past. A great way to get into the moment is to continuously ask yourself, *If these are the last five minutes of my life, is this what I want to be experiencing?* This simple question can get us into the moment, and most importantly help us to choose the most satisfying experience in such a moment.

In the State of Gray, we are fully aware of our minds and our bodies. We become the ruler of our minds, versus being ruled by our minds. The State of Gray is becoming aware of how our bodies feel, and consciously releasing any tension, anxiety, and pain. It is becoming aware of the stories of our left brain, and setting them aside so we can truly be in the moment. Being in the State of Gray is the core of true existence. It is like our naked bodies without the trappings of any clothes or makeup. It is our bare essential Type Me. It is the truth without our story. It is where the truth exists without perception and judgment. And it is an incredible place of peace, joy, and contentment.

Being in the State of Gray is difficult to describe because it is different than most of the feelings we experience throughout the day. In fact, it is more of an "un-feeling." Being in the State of Gray removes us from the cares and concerns of this world. It is not a state of apathy, but a deep peace and contentment. The State of Gray is being released from our to-do's, our worries, and from everything we deem important in our daily lives. For just a few moments, we can be without the trappings of our lives. When we are released from our earthly concerns, we are able to experience how it is to just be. We are aware of and can feel each sensation in our entire body. Our senses are heightened, and we can consciously seek out discomfort in our bodies and gently release it. In the State of Gray, our minds are at rest. Similar to the state we are in just before we fall asleep or as we awaken, a soft, calming ethereal haze envelops us. We lose our sense of self, our role, our duties, and our ego. Being in the State of Gray, we return to our true selves without the façade of the life we have created. The State of Gray brings us back into our bodies, our feelings, and our authentic selves.

Personally, I use a meditation or guided imagery recording to ease myself into the State of Gray. Concentrating on the audio keeps my mind occupied and helps me release my mental monkey chatter. I close my eyes, breathe deeply from my abdomen, and scan my body for tenseness to be released. I ease deeper and deeper into my breath. If you have ever been in hypnosis, the State of Gray is similar to the dreamlike state a hypnotist helps you into just before going into the full hypnotic state. My body begins to feel hollow. I can feel the skin and outer wrappings of my physical body but the insides feel vacant and peaceful. With an empty mind, an empty body, and ever deepening breathing, I relax completely. After losing myself in the State of Gray for fifteen to twenty minutes, I slowly rejoin the world. Just like waking in the morning, I stretch and open my eyes, slowly rejoining the world feeling refreshed and replenished.

The State of Gray *is a place of being, not of doing.* As a recovering Type A, the concept of *not doing* was foreign and terrifying to me. In the beginning, I could release my stories and stop the spiral of mental monkey chatter, but the idea of taking a few moments to do nothing was unthinkable. How could I? So much needed to be accomplished. As I write this paragraph, my to-do list includes: finishing my book, finding an editor, taking care of my clients, posting my next workshops online, attending networking functions, finding a new doctor for my great aunt, going to the grocery store, returning a dress, and taking my mother to her weekly appointment. And those are just the things I can think of off the top of my head. It does not include all of the emails I still need to respond to, and the rest of the projects I could begin. Take time to clear my mind? What a waste.

Well, not really. It is against all logic, but taking the time to clear one's mind is actually the key to productivity. Think about it. If you wake up in the morning and immediately start on your laundry list of to-do's, you are already behind the eight ball. You have created a story where you are ruled by doing, by completing, by tasks. When the tasks seem overwhelming, don't get done, or take up so much of your day you can't breathe, where is the joy? When I take fifteen minutes in the morning and fully place myself into the State of Gray, my mind clears. All of a sudden, ways to make my tasks easier and more efficient pop into mind. Some less-important tasks naturally fall off my to-do list or are taken care of by others. At my core, I am a tried-and-true organizational freak, and I know better than anyone there is no logical explanation for being more productive by taking time to "do nothing," but time and again I see it is true.

Jennifer lived more by her checklists than I ever did. She was a single mother who worked full time, had a side business, and was very involved in local community organizations. From the moment she woke up to the second she fell asleep, her day was programmed down to the minute with a list of tasks to complete. She depended on this list. Without it, she was terrified something would fall through the cracks. Jennifer did not take well to the State of Gray. She could not find time to schedule it into her day. If she did try to get into the State of Gray, she spent the time mentally reviewing her checklist. Together we found ways to ease her into the State of Gray. First, I recommended Jennifer use mealtime as State of Gray reminders. She was to take three deep from-the-belly breaths before every meal and to refrain from doing anything else but eat until the meal was complete. Through this experience, she was able to let go, just a bit. Her mealtime became a haven for her. In time, she found that yoga was another way she could let go of her daily concerns and focus on one thing. As the State of Gray became part of her life, the dependency on her list loosened, and so did how she experienced her day. She is just as busy and just as productive, if not more so, but she can do it now with a smile. Jennifer's days are less harried, less structured, and more flexible. And now her side business is thriving, and she is enjoying more of her life.

The concept of the State of Gray is very simple and straight-forward, but it also can be very challenging to execute. The first homework I give to all of my clients is both the simplest assignment and the most difficult. I ask them to practice being in the State of Gray for fifteen minutes every day. This means no talking, no thinking, no imagining, no listening, no eating, no moving, and no nothing. Pretty simple, huh? Well, I would say at least 90 percent of my clients have difficulty with it. They cannot find fifteen minutes a day for themselves. Like Jennifer, they feel it is a waste of time when they have so much else to do. They can't stop the left-brain monkey chatter for even a few minutes. Honestly, it has taken me years to do this more consistently, and still on some stressful days, it is challenging to get into the gray zone. But I also know firsthand how important the State of Gray is.

When I was first introduced to and tried to enter the State of Gray, I was an extreme Type A existing solely on stress. Sitting in lotus position and meditating for hours was unimaginable. Honestly, I still can't. Luckily we have many ways to achieve a State of Gray, and meditation is just one of them. You can also strengthen your right brain through yoga, guided imagery, conscious breathing, chanting, self-hypnosis, prayer, or any activity that gives your left brain a rest. If your monkey chatter and stress levels are high, find some activities that occupy your mind just enough to keep it busy, but not frantic. When I am too crazed to quiet myself into meditation, one of my favorite ways to unplug is to play solitaire. Solitaire is just enough thinking and enough routine to occupy my left brain, allowing more space for my right brain to breathe. Other people have found success through knitting, running, and other forms of repetitive movement. Be a kid. Get lost in something creative like coloring or humming your favorite song. Try different techniques until you find the one that works for you, and then practice it at least once a day for fifteen minutes or more.

Thousands of books and programs have been written about how to reach the State of Gray. Do some research to find the best technique for you. When clients have a hard time finding a practice, I recommend starting with quiet time in the car. Everyone drives everywhere these days. Use that time to be in the State of Gray. Turn off the radio and your mobile phone. Just concentrate on the act of driving. Be hyper-aware of the road, the lights, the other cars. Release the judgments you are making about how fast or slow traffic is, or about the skills of the other drivers. Be aware of your body. Relax any tension in your shoulders. Notice any thoughts that come into your mind, and release them without judgment. Release any worries or concerns. Nothing exists in this moment except for you in the act of driving.

Another way I enter the State of Gray is by choosing a random item, for instance, a leaf. I look at the leaf, a unique leaf on a full tree. I study the leaf, tracing the veins running through its soft, papery surface. Perhaps small bug bites are apparent in one section. I study how the colors on either side of the leaf are different, or how the hint of fall has begun to brown its edges. Once I have fully seen all the details of the single leaf, I expand my vision to the grouping of leaves it is connected with, then the section of the branch to which it is attached, and finally I expand my view to see it as part of the whole tree. With each expansion of my vision, I take the time to see every detail I can about a particular section. The unique leaf still remains present, but I can see how it is also just one section, one unit of the tree—a unique identity, but also a component of something larger. In taking this moment to reconnect to the intricate details of life, recognizing how all parts lead to the whole, I am released from the blindness of anxiety, and I relax into the current moment. I reach a State of Gray.

Whatever practice you choose to find your State of Gray, the practice should have three key components: turn off, release, and surrender.

- **First, turn off all outside stimulation.** There should be no visual, audio, or tactile stimulation. Find a place where you can be without distraction. Unplug in a secluded, quiet area where you will not be disturbed. If your State of Gray is a practice like running or driving, mentally focus only on the task at hand. Keep your mind from wandering or judging.
- **The next step is to release.** Scan your body for pain and tightness. Consciously release this tension. Become aware of your breathing, and relax your breath to slow down your bodily systems. Nothing is really needed from your body right now, so shut down everything non-essential. Allow your body to be comfortable and at rest. Release your ego, your left brain, and your mental monkey chatter. Release all thought from your mind. If you cannot fully release, release your necessity to do so. Release as much as you can and be content.
- **Finally, surrender.** Just be. Exist without your judgments. Allow yourself to fall into a space of calm quiet. Think of it as the mental equivalent of floating in salt water. Like floating in water, the more you try to float, the less you can float. By

focusing consciously on your breathing, you can relax into the support of a chair or the earth. Let go of all desire to *make* yourself supported, and just *allow* yourself to be supported. Relax into your breath and let go, knowing you are supported. Just be. Nothing else needs to be done.

To me, how you get to a State of Gray is not as important as experiencing and integrating the State of Gray into your life. Build up to at least fifteen minutes a day. Make it a routine. Make it a habit. Make it so you truly miss it if you have to skip a day. As you come to know what it feels like to be in the State of Gray, be more aware throughout your day. When do you feel most like the State of Gray, and when do you feel yourself being pulled into stress and strain created by perception and judgment? Be aware of how your levels of joy and productivity align with the amount of time you spend in the State of Gray. How much time do you need to spend there? How does your life improve when you include this foundational tool?

As you begin to be more comfortable with the State of Gray, try to integrate it into your daily activities. In addition to breaking out fifteen minutes for focused Gray, add in pops of Gray when you are stressed. Take a few deep breaths before a big board meeting. Count to ten before responding to a difficult person. Add reminders throughout your day to pop into the State of Gray. See how being centered in this state, and breaking free of the frantic desire to do, can help improve your stress levels, productivity, and clarity and bring you back into Awareness.

FINDING THE TRUE CAUSE

Our modern world is focused on symptoms. We look for relief from the pain we experience, or the issue we see. We are not focused on the cause behind the problem. When I was going through my medical issues, the doctors all focused on my symptoms. They searched for ways to reduce the pain. They looked to pills or surgery to improve my digestion and menstrual cycle. What they didn't do was uncover *why* I was having problems. They sought to make my pain manageable, but did nothing to help uncover *why* it was happening. Even in working with the alternative healers, the focus was on healing the pain, not ensuring it would not happen again. When I returned from Peru and saw how quickly my pain returned, I knew I had not found a solution to my problem, just temporary relief from my symptoms. Type-Me Habits are focused on uncovering and treating the causes of the pain. When the causes are resolved, the symptoms will also be released.

We often blame others and circumstances for our symptoms. We blame our job, our spouse, our childhood, our DNA, or the economy for our stress. We see the source of our problem outside of our self. We believe we are victims of these outside factors. The key to the Type-Me Habits is accepting our pain is not the result of any of these situations, or anything outside of us. Our pain is due to our reaction and beliefs about what is happening around us. The answer to alleviating our stress is to fix our thinking, actions, reactions, and beliefs. The answer is not anything outside of us; it is within.

The past is perception. The future is unknown. The only truth is the present. Being in the State of Gray brings us to the present. In the present, we can find the truth. When we are fully in the moment, we can be aware of what we are truly experiencing. We can check in with the state of our mind. We can notice the effectiveness of our bodies. We can perceive our feeling, spiritual, intuitive state. We notice what feels good, and what feels painful.

The next step is investigating the *why* we are experiencing what we are. We need to first notice we are experiencing heart-burn, and then we need to decipher if our heartburn is because of the pepperoni pizza we had for lunch, or if it is because of the upcoming business meeting. It is important we don't judge our-selves ("It was stupid of me to have pepperoni. I know it bothers my stomach"), but simply to compile data. We can't change what has just happened, but we can change our choices for the future.

Often in life we look at the *symptoms* of our pain, instead of the *cause*. It makes sense we are aware of the symptoms because it's where we *feel* our pain. However, the symptoms are just there to grab our attention. Once we are aware of our symptoms, aware something is not right, it is time to uncover the true cause of the pain.

Heather had an issue with a co-worker. The discussion started in the world of emotions. It centered around what Heather felt, what she was experiencing, and the belief it was her co-work-er's responsibility to affect what Heather was experiencing. She was completely focused on the pain she felt, and the perception of how wrongly she was treated. She wanted her co-worker to know the pain she was feeling. She was trapped and clouded by emotion. She was trapped in her story. I had Heather release her story, and how she felt. After we put it aside, we explored why this incident was so painful for her. Why did it mean so much to her? The truth was Heather liked her co-worker, and she was concerned the co-worker was not aware of how his actions were being received by others. When we removed her emotions, and found the true source of her pain, we were able to uncover the ac-tionable steps to help the co-worker improve his communication skills. The emotional pain my client was experiencing was only the *symptom* to alert her to help the true *cause*, her co-worker's poor communication skills.

Another client, Roy, told me about a fight with his wife about the holidays. He went on and on about all the details of the fight: the logistics of their separate holidays, the unfairness of his spouse keeping him from his family, and the bossiness of his wife's demands. If I tried to resolve all the perceptions and issues Roy presented, we would not have solved the true problem. The true cause of this disagreement was because both Roy and his wife felt insecure about their relationship. What they needed was more trust, understanding, communication, and unconditional love. Resolving the details of the holiday fight would have never fixed the true cause deep inside them both.

Here are a few steps I take with my clients to find the cause of their pain so actionable steps can be taken to bring them back to their right space.

- **Stop.** As explained in the State of Gray, the first step is to stop in order to gain distance and objectivity. When we are in the midst of the pain, confusion, and emotions, we cannot act clearly. Step aside. Walk away. Turn off. Tune in. Give yourself some physical, emotional, and psychological distance from the perceived source of your pain. This does not need to be a lot of time, but you do need to be completely removed from the situation. It is necessary to step far enough away so you no longer are exposed to or responsive to the source of pain.
- **Take Out the Emotion.** To help you have clear objectivity on the issue, it is necessary to first clear out all the emotion. Emotion can be a symptom alerting us to unrest, but it is not the cause, and it tends to cloud our thinking. Emotion needs to be removed in order to see the truth of the situation. Journal, punch a pillow, cry, go for a run, or whatever you need to do to release your emotions in a healthy way.
- **Remove the Us-Versus-Them Mentality.** When we are in our pain, we tend to make it us-versus-them. We make

the other the source of our pain, when in fact they may be innocent bystanders. Remove any blame toward the other. They are not causing your pain. Our pain is caused by our own beliefs, actions, or reactions. When we release any blame toward the other, we are empowered to see the true cause of our pain.

• **What Can You Affect?** Focus only on what you can truly affect. We cannot change things in the past, others' beliefs, or some circumstances. Look within your own realm regarding what you can affect. Dig down to the actionable issues. Don't focus on fixing emotions, symptoms of your being off-track, or anything you cannot affect. How are you able to affect the true facts of the situation?

• **What Can the Other Affect?** Also look clearly at what the other person can do. They are not responsible and cannot take away your emotional pain. Like you, they can only affect their own beliefs, actions, and reactions. Be aware of trying to make the other responsible for things outside of their reach.

• **Take Action.** Look at your needs, the needs of others, the requirements of a circumstance, and the truth of the situation. What are the tangible, actionable steps you can take? We will explore this step more in-depth in the chapter on Alternatives. For now, we are going to delve more deeply into growing our awareness of symptoms and true causes experienced in our mind, body, and spirit.

PULL YOURSELF BACK TOGETHER

When I returned from Peru, I had initially thought my healing was all due to the mystical shamanic rituals, which included strong mind-altering plant medicines. But it was due to becoming aware of my truth. I had become aware of what made me happy—and what did not. I became in touch with my authentic, true self, my Type Me, not the person I thought I had to be, or the person I assumed everyone else was. I had identified me, what works specifically for me, and embraced what I uniquely need. My Type Me is not what my family or society says I should be. It is not how my career or family roles dictate I should act. It is not what my fear of ridicule or poverty says I should be. It is not what one or another doctor told me was best for me to eat or do. It was not what different people professed was the only way to find peace and joy. My Type Me is the truth of who I am at my core. When I am feeding my Type Me what it wants, I am happy, joyful, and peaceful. When I do not give my Type Me what it desires, I am stressed, ill, and depressed.

My Type Me exists at the intersection of my individual mental, emotional, psychological, and physical needs. Throughout my trip to Peru, I set cognitive intentions for my good health, and every day I wrote in my journal to sort through the rambling misperceptions of my mind. The staff took care of everything, which released me from any responsibility, and therefore any control-freak stress I would have otherwise experienced. Plus I went alone, which released me from my codependent tendencies. These releases freed me from the prison of my to-do's, shoulds and have-to's, allowing me to reconnect with my soul. I finally had space to allow my spirit to explore what I truly wanted.

I was surrounded by ancient miracles and beautiful vistas, and they fed my Type Me. My body was cleansed through the month-long preparation without alcohol, caffeine, sugar, and spicy foods, plus doing a mineral water cleansing removed any remaining gunk in my digestive system. The muscular and respiratory systems of my body were also in the best shape they had been in years due to all the walking I did in preparation for the trip. The shamanic energy work cleared up years of debris clogging my spirit. The plant medicine allowed me to experience a pure right-brain connection with all. No specific one of these individual elements provided the healing, but the combination of them. Not one aspect of me affected my healing more than the others. It took working on all the aspects of me to provide the state of wellbeing I desired. I was healed by being aware of and in balance with all of my Type Me's needs.

To understand our world, we often break it down into separate concepts. The same holds true to understand our *self.* We tend to separate each part of our self into our mind, body, and spirit so we can discuss their different functions and needs, but the division is only semantics. Our mind is in our brain, which is part of our body. Our spirit affects our perceptions, and also the state of our internal bodily systems. What we put into our bodies can affect the working of our minds. The interplay between mind, body, and spirit is seamless. These aspects of *self* are not separate, but overlapping systems. Our left brain loves to categorize things: "This is a hat. This is a broach. This is a pterodactyl." But a name is just a name. It is a concept created by a person trying to explain the world around them, as well as each particular item's role. The more something is important to us, the more names, labels, and divisions we give it. A boat is just a boat, but my husband can categorize boats by make, model, year, engine, hull type, usage, and perhaps fifty other factors. When we name something, we put it into one of our pretty little left-brain file folders. There it sits isolated, but it is not truly detached. It is part of an integrated whole. All aspects of our being are very interrelated; they are separate and yet one in the same. It is important to think of one's self in wholeness, not separation.

Street directions are not my forte. When I drive into Chicago, it is often a challenge. Over the years, I have come to know some neighborhoods. I know different ways to reach Wrigley Field,

Shakespeare Repertory Theatre, and Grant Park. But ask me where they are all located in relation to the city, or how to get from one to the other, and I am lost. One day I was absolutely amazed. Due to traffic and construction, I was taken off my usual route, and I bumped into another part of town I knew. I was floored. The two sections were only blocks apart. I had no idea. I think the same is true for the parts of us. We try to neatly organize, separate, and compartmentalize the different parts of us, when they really bump up next to each other, and more probably overlap. Just like we can separate different attractions in Chicago, or see them all as part of what makes up the city, the same is true for us. We can see ourselves as separated, unrelated parts, or as a whole interrelated system.

Think of the ocean. Looking out at the vast body of water, one can define it all as ocean. But change your focus and see each wave. Now focus even closer and look at each droplet of water in each wave in the ocean. We can see and name each of these elements: droplet, wave, and ocean. We can continue to break the ocean into smaller and smaller units until we can see the two hydrogen atoms bonded to an oxygen atom, which together make up each droplet of water. We can also move things out further. Start with water droplets, which create waves; groups of waves make the tide; the tide makes up the Santa Maria Bay, which can extend to the Sea of Cortez, and even out to the Pacific Ocean and beyond. The only difference between any of this is where we decide to focus. Whether it is a unique section or part of a whole is a matter of perspective. Depending on what is important, we can choose to focus on different parts of the ocean. For instance, looking at individual water droplets through a microscope would not be helpful if a large tidal wave were coming at us. We need a different focus at different times.

The same is true for the aspects of us. If we are hungry, we need to eat, not meditate for twelve hours. If our mind is cloudy, a brisk walk, not more thinking, can unclog it. Focusing too much on any one aspect can keep us stuck, or keep us from finding the relief we need. It is important to be aware of and balance the three aspects of us. In my case, I need to actively disengage my mind so I can become aware of the needs of my body and spirit. I know of people who are really spiritual, but they are so removed from their minds they have difficulty remembering to pay their bills. Others are so engrossed in their bodies they spend all their time focused on diet, exercise, and appearance, and they miss out on the peace provided through spirit or the exhilaration of engaging the mind.

When I was ill, the medical professionals focused on only one part or system of me, missing the true cause of my illness. By only looking at one organ or bodily system, they were blinded. For instance, one doctor was trained to only look at my digestive system, but didn't take into account how it was affected by my menstrual cycle. As I looked at how each of my bodily systems interacted with each other, how they were also affected by what I put into my body, the thoughts of my mind, and my emotional state, I began to understand the full meaning of health.

It is important to be aware of how all of these systems are interrelated and affect each other. As a young child, my eyesight was very poor. Anything more than six inches from my nose was out of focus. To me, the world looked like one massive Monet painting, varying shapes and colors blurring into each other, and making up a patchwork landscape. Nothing was distinct. Nothing was crisp. Nothing had definition. In third grade, I received my first pair of glasses. The optometrist did not prescribe glasses to provide twenty/twenty vision as he was trying to correct my strong astigmatism. The lenses allowed me to see the chalkboard, but not much else.

So even with glasses, I was left in this world of softened images. My world of imperfect vision kept me distanced from others. I did not see the world they did, so I could not share in their experiences. My clouded, hazy shadow world distanced me from others, kept me from experiencing a full life. I missed so much in life because it was all blended together. I didn't notice details because I couldn't see them. My only refuge was to turn inward.

Finally after thirteen years living in a world that fell out of focus once it passed my nose, I was fitted with the right prescription, allowing me to see the rest of the world blocked from me for so long. I remember leaving the optometrist's office and stopping in my tracks. For the first time, I could see each individual leaf on the tree outside. I could see each unique brick on the building across the street. It was as if I had stepped into a whole new world. This was an exciting world, with so much detail to see in every moment. I could see people's facial reactions when I was speaking to them. I could notice intricate details in art. Beautiful images formed in how colors and shapes and textures worked together. I began to feel connected to others. I began to leave my inner world, the only one I could access before, and I began to experience the larger world.

I am grateful for my gift of sight, and also for my gift of blindness. Blindness allowed me to become more in tune to my intuition and my inner sense. The gift of sight opened my eyes to the world outside of me, to the details, differences, uniqueness, and interconnection of people, cultures, and nature. Our physical state can affect how we see the world, and changing one's physical being can affect one's perspective and experience. It can also work the other way around. My client, Amy, wanted to lose weight, but she was not able to commit to a change in diet and exercise until we first worked through the blocks in her mind. Amy is a very determined woman who had the power to stick to exercise and diet programs. She would adhere rigidly to a thirty-day program, but once it was over, she returned to her old habits. The problem was not willpower. She had power in spades. We explored together what health, weight, food, and exercise meant to her on a deep emotional level. I asked her why she was afraid of losing weight, and what she gained by having extra weight. We discovered, to her, weight meant protection from harm, and food meant love. Once Amy released these beliefs, and chose new beliefs about safety and love, she was able to make permanent changes to her current physical state, and to stick to a new lifestyle.

Mind, body, and spirit affect each other. Sometimes we need to address one area before we can go after another. When I was at my lowest point, I needed to receive some physical relief from the pain before I could begin to do the work to uncover the mental and spiritual causes of my dis-ease.

We are like a three-legged stool. No matter how strong two of the legs are, if the third is broken, it is impossible for the stool to be stable and useful. The same is true for us. No matter how strong my mind and spirit, if I stop exercising, and at the same time fill my belly with synthetic, unnatural foods, it is only a matter of time before my ailing body will begin to bring down my mind and spirit. For a joyous, wonderful life, it is important to take care of all the things making up our personal Type Me. In order to take care of our own three-legged stool of complete health, it is necessary to be aware of if and how we are in alignment mind, body, and soul.

WHAT ARE YOU THINKING?

What we say, think, and believe dictates what we experience. Unfortunately much of what we believe, think, and say is done unconsciously. The goal is to bring the realm of our unconscious thoughts to our Awareness so we can make conscious choices about how we experience our day.

One place to expand your Awareness is in your word choice. A few clues to look for in your everyday language can hint at the black-and-white programming you need to uninstall.

• First is to listen for **over-generalizations**, which are usually preceded by "always" or "never." For example, you may say, "I am *always* late" or "I *never* make it anywhere on time."

• Second, watch for **absolutes**. These binding statements include "should" or "have to." They may apply to us, "I *have* to finish all my laundry this evening, or I am a slob," or they may extend our judgment on to others, "A good mother *should* be early when she picks up her children from soccer practice." Other watchwords in the absolute category are "no one" and "everyone." "No one" usually shows up when we are playing the victim. "No one ever asks me how I am." Using "everyone" assumes we have only one universal and acceptable way to do something. "Everyone knows the best cars come from Germany." These words point out the expectations we have for others, and for our self. Most times these expectations are our own creation, but we take them as universal law.

• **Premonitions** are a third indicator of black-and-white thinking. "I was *almost* killed today when a car merged into my lane." "I *could have* caught a cold with everyone sniffling at work." The funny thing about these statements is our mind experiences them as reality. We don't register the "almost" or "could have," and instead feel the same intensity and pain as if they truly occurred. The amygdala in our brain is so vigilant in protecting us, it not only senses real physical danger, but it also takes our thoughts as an expression of reality, and kicks in to protect us when we are just *think* something *might* happen. We will explore our brain and how it affects our experience later in this book, but for now, it is important to know that what we think is what we experience, so it is important to become aware of our thoughts.

- **Labeling** is the last language sign. Labeling moves us away from fact into judgment. Instead of saying, "I made a mistake," we label ourselves by saying "I *am* an idiot." Labeling is where we jump to conclusions, usually negative ones, so our mind can categorize and classify the situation or individuals involved, even ourselves. Another way to label is to add adjectives. Note when you are adding derogatory, attacking, or minimizing adjectives to yourself or others.

Below are some examples of everyday conversations. Can you catch *perception* creeping into reality through the word choices?

- Bob is livid with his co-worker Gary. "*Everyone* knows it is important to complete the TPS reports with a blue pen, not a black pen. Using a blue pen is the *proper* way to fill out the report. I can't believe how *stupid* and *inconsiderate* Gary is. And it is *so unfair* he gets away with it."
- Susie has a tendency to focus on the negative. "You won't believe what happened yesterday. Some *jerk* pulled out in front of me and *almost* hit me! I *could* have been *killed!*" (But Susie, you weren't hit, right?) "Yes, but I *could* have been! I can't believe what a *bad* driver he was. They shouldn't let *idiots* like him get a license."
- Matt is trying to buy a new house. "I don't know where to start. I'm just *not smart* about these things. I will *probably* be taken advantage of because I am so *dumb.*"

Did you find the not-so-hidden black-and-white thinking above? Now the challenge is to find it in your own life, and your own words. Our words reflect our beliefs and deep assumptions. If we can be aware of what we express, we can begin to uncover our beliefs, and decide whether they serve us. Remember, no action needs to be taken at this time. Just begin to grow your awareness. Use this awareness to begin to realize how what you experience is affected by your perceptions, as well as the stories you tell yourself.

YOUR BODY IS SPEAKING TO YOU

Being aware of our bodies takes two forms. First are messages regarding the way we choose to treat our bodies, which in turn affects our experience of life. Second are messages from our bodies about the situations we are experiencing.

Let's first explore how we treat our bodies. When I was having all of my menstrual issues, I felt defective. The doctors reinforced this by trying to find what was wrong with me to cause my issues. They looked to diagnose, prescribe, and perform surgery to fix a broken body. They looked at my symptoms and suggested trying medicines or removing parts of my body to fix the symptoms. But it is like trying to fix a damaged wall. The wall can be patched and repaired, but if the source of the damage, say a leak, is never investigated and repaired, no amount of patching will ever fix the wall. The doctors only looked at repairing the wall to remove my pain, and never investigated the cause of the pain.

When I prepared to visit Peru, I was on a very strict diet. This included no caffeine. Caffeine had always been my constant companion. Mountain Dew was my drink of choice in my high school and college days. Once I entered the world of work, coffee became my mainstay. It was a challenge to give up this addiction and crutch, but I did. What I noticed after my trip, and therefore after six weeks without caffeine, was my menstrual cycle improved. I also noticed as I reintroduced caffeine into my system, the issues returned. My body was not broken. It was not something to fix. I was simply filling it with something not agreeable to my personal body system. Remove the caffeine; remove the issues.

Nothing was wrong with me. I didn't have a defect. I didn't have an undiagnosed ailment. I was simply putting something detrimental into my body. Our bodies are perfect. They are amazing machines, but when we choose to give them substances that do not work in our unique system, or deny our bodies of what they do need, the machine malfunctions. By becoming aware of how certain foods affect my body, good or bad, I understand the repercussions of my decisions. I am then able to make choices about what I consume, and I am empowered to control my health by being aware of how my body is affected by foods, exercise, and toxins around and in me.

Become a detective of your own body. Remove frequently consumed foods for a period of two months and note any changes in your body's performance. Slowly add foods/liquids back one at a time, and notice any physiological changes. Keep a food journal, and note how you feel after consuming certain foods. Sometimes certain foods create an immediate reaction due to a food allergy, and sometimes it is the quantity consumed over time that causes a reaction. Take the time to do the research on your own body. See how many of your ailments you can affect with simple diet change. Research Hindu Ayurvedic medicine, blood type, or other diets based on unique body types. Make the suggestions they recommend, and see which suggestions improve your health. Uncover the power you have to affect your body before resorting to medicine or surgery. Take back your health, and be your own doctor.

The other part of body awareness is the signals our body sends us about what is good or bad for us. Our bodies can alert us to not only what is good or bad for our bodily systems, but can also provide input about situations we are in, or people who are around us. Have you ever walked down a dark alley and felt the hairs on your arm raise? This is your body warning of danger. Our bodies speak to us throughout the day. It is our job to begin to hear and listen to them. Begin to be aware of the signals and messages your body is sending you. My body has always spoken to me. It just took me a long time to understand what it was saying.

When I was younger, I was fortunate enough to go to summer camp. During the week, we did crafts and took lessons in all kinds of interesting things. At the end of each week was a big social event, a dance, or an awards ceremony, which all the campers anticipated. Throughout the years and after a series of camps, I consistently had a 100-degree fever on the evening of the big event. However, I usually was not upset about missing the event. The truth was, large crowds made me uncomfortable. I thoroughly enjoyed the one-to-one contact during the week, but being in a big social group was not my thing. I felt I was deficient in some manner because I preferred not to participate. So my body helped me be true to myself, and provided me with a way to avoid such a situation. The day after the event, the fever was gone, and I was content and happy.

During high school and college I constantly worked at my schoolwork, theater, and after-school jobs. Without fail, when we had spring or winter break, I always developed a debilitating cold. Instead of working at the shopping mall or reading up for the next semester, I was down for the count. My body and mind were worn out. I felt I needed to keep working, even when everyone else was taking a break, so my body shut down, and I was forced to relax and recharge. My body forced me to get what I truly needed.

Often our minds tell us what we must do or have to do, even when these things are not true to our Type Me, so our bodies step in. Whenever we have a headache, backache, or stomachache, our knee-jerk reaction is to grab a pill or have surgery to relieve our pain. But what if we stopped and first investigated the source of the pain? Yes, sometimes a stomachache is just some bad chow mein. But if your stomach constantly hurts after the quarterly meeting, Thanksgiving with the in-laws, or the PTA meeting, it may be a sign something is "not right" in your daily life.

For me personally, the diseases I experienced were not always a medical condition, but dis-ease with my life. Our minds and thoughts reflect what society tells us should be, or what we should do. Unfortunately, many times those messages are counter to what we are really meant to do. Stop and listen to your body. The body is in touch with your essential self, with your true self, with your Type Me. Become aware of your body's messages, and how they reflect your true needs.

A HEALTHY DOSE OF SOUL FOOD

What feeds your soul, and are you getting enough of it? Your soul food might mean attending a religious service or practice, but it may also mean a walk in nature, reading a good book, admiring something beautiful like a painting, listening to music, creating something unique, or playing your favorite sport. Be a detective and uncover your personal soul food. Things you do to feed your soul may not be logical or profitable, but you find great joy in them. If it's hard to explain why you can't get enough of something, and your friends think what brings you joy is strange, you have probably found what feeds your soul.

Harry had a challenging job and thought he needed to make a change because he was usually feeling drained, down, and depressed. However, when November came around he was energized, creative, joyful, and happy. Every year Harry participated in National Novel Writing Month where the participants are challenged to write an entire book in one month. Harry loves to write. It is his soul food. If our work together were simply to help him find a new job, it would *not* have solved the problem of his lethargy. The way for Harry to feel better every day was to integrate writing into his Daily Habits so he could feed his soul more often.

Many of us deny our soul foods because they seem frivolous. Common work ethics prohibit many of us from taking time to enjoy life, participate in joy-producing activities, or to allow ourselves a little "me time." Remember, our spirit is also an important part of who we are. Give as much attention to your soul food as to your relationship with your body and mind. To find true joy, you must feed your soul and spirit with what it desires.

After identifying a few of your *soul foods*, determine how often you need to experience them, and what happens if it has been too long between experiencing your soul food. Uncover what is keeping you from doing it more often, such as fear, time, didn't believe it was important, anticipated ridicule, putting others first, etc. Note what happens when you re-integrate your soul food into your life.

All too often we walk blindly through our lives and feel like the victim of circumstances. Awareness puts us back into the driver's seat. By being a detective of our own words, thoughts, beliefs, actions, reactions, body, and spirit, we can uncover the causes of our pain, stress, and discontent. Without this Awareness, we have no way to make positive changes in our lives because we do not know what needs to be changed. Take time to be in the

State of Gray, growing your ability to be centered, and therefore more able to be a non-judgmental detective. The next few pages following my client's story contain tools to help you grow your current Awareness and maintain strong Awareness each and every day. Integrate the best working Habits for you into your Daily Practice.

CLIENT'S TYPE-ME STORY: THERE ARE NO COINCIDENCES

By Roni Weiner Pressler

Growth from within, and the growth spurt I made while studying with Melissa, stems from the realization there are no coincidences. For me, the revelation I received from my work with her was paramount. I remember the day it happened, and it changed forever how I thought about what goes on around us. It has made me aware of what I should be noticing, and what others so often miss. You can almost see it in people who don't notice; they aren't aware they just missed something big. You want to say to them, "Do you know what just happened?" You can't because they won't see it anyway, but I try not to miss those things in my own life now.

Several times a day, I say silently or out loud, "You know there are no coincidences." It has become my mantra. This part of me wasn't there before we worked together, and it changed me totally in how I view and think about my daily interactions. Coincidences are not weird, ironic, or unexpected events. Coincidences are fortunate opportunities—Spectacularly Perfect Events, as Melissa says. I no longer think, "What an amazing coincidence!" Instead I think, "What happened was supposed to happen, so I need to not miss what I am supposed to be getting from this."

If you think of everything as just random coincidences, then you are a powerless pawn to meaningless events. If, instead, you believe there are no coincidences, then you know fortune just came to you. After I had been laid off due to downsizing, I thought a series of events was random. Three days after I was let go, I had to go near my old office for a doctor's appointment and then lunch with a friend. To fill the few hours in between, I planned to camp out at Starbucks with my laptop. As I was sitting there, several people I knew through my previous position came in, so it was one conversation after another. I didn't realize at the time it was not a coincidence to run into all of them, or to feel their supportive friendship surrounding me. They kept telling me encouraging things about my transition: "You were so overqualified for your job." "Something better is going to come along." "You know you could always come back and work at the hospital." "You know you could do a million and one things." This was the support and encouragement I needed after an unexpected layoff.

Interestingly, one of my closest friends was in Starbucks and upon hearing my story said, "I listen to you, and you seem really happy and really content. But people who have had the same job for twenty-five years, and then get let go without notice, shouldn't be as happy as you are now. So I want you to know this is going to change." Those things were very helpful to hear, because when my happiness did fade, I remembered his words, and wasn't so surprised by my feelings.

I also ran into George at Starbucks. From across the room our eyes met, and he pointed at me and said, "I've been thinking about you." At the time, I thought it odd to run into him after not seeing him for five years, and I wondered, *Why was he thinking about me?* As it turned out, he wanted me to work on a new project he was involved in, and I left our meeting thinking running into him was just a weird coincidence. Since then, George and I have become very good friends while working on his project. Understanding the truth about Spectacularly Perfect Events like running into my supporters, being given the gift of insight from my close friend, and seeing George was all lost on me. I didn't start working with Melissa until six weeks later. However, in a few weeks, the whole realization of "no coincidences" came about between us, and the whole earlier day began to *make sense*. Understanding there are no coincidences was pivotal for my life. Had I not met Melissa, I am positive I would still be unaware of all the support I received—all the angels who appeared, as she put it—and the true gift of my friendship with George.

Because I know there are no coincidences, I don't miss opportunities. My new awareness makes the difficult moments easier, and the happy moments happier, because I am aware. Being aware makes me live, as she says, in my perfect life or it makes me happier in the life I am in, because I am not missing anything. I think so many people are missing much of what is happening to them. Being hyper-aware allows me to see what they are missing. Sometimes I feel like I am seeing situations as I stand outside of them, even though I am experiencing them. I can see clearly, completely, expansively, and intricately all at the same time. I can see where I am, and where I am coming from. I can see what others are believing and experiencing. I can see what others are missing. I see things I could not see before. I am aware of my actions and emotions in a new way. It makes me multifaceted, if you will, taking me out of the act of doing and into a state of awareness. This heightened state of awareness provides the opportunities to choose options not apparent before.

A few years ago I had a series of discussions with a friend wherein we identified two views of life on earth. Our debate centered on two possible options: 1) Are we all marionettes, and somebody is just pulling our strings? or, 2) Do we choose our lives and make our own decisions? Now I feel very certain because there are no coincidences, another choice exists. What we are presented with are planned situations created by a higher power, allowing us to make the choices with which we then live. Earlier at Starbucks, I could have said to George, "No, I'm not interested," and the experience of us working together and our renewed friendship would not have happened. My growth, both professionally and personally, would just not be there. The opportunity presented itself, but it was up to me to choose to take it. Because I chose it, it created a whole different set of opportunities and experiences. It has been helpful in a thousand ways. I don't know if it would have been a bad thing not to choose it, but it was clearly a choice. Awareness and choice are what give us control in our lives, and the reason we are not all the same. I don't think we are marionettes, but I do think we are presented with lots of opportunities. People who think these events are just coincidences often miss the opportunities they present.

I now see the world attached to an intricate plan where we have a choice, and the choice we make creates our path. A game plan does exist, but we decide how we approach it. George made a choice when he walked into Starbucks. We won't ever know what would have happened if he didn't need coffee then. But he did choose to get coffee from the same location, and when he saw me, he chose to come and tell me about his project. I also made a momentary decision, and so we connected. In the beginning, I was focused on the opportunity of the project, but now the journey seems more important than the outcome. So often our most valuable lessons are seen in our rearview mirror, but I know no matter what happens to our project, George and I will remain friends forever.

Another concept that took me a while to understand came when Melissa tried to help me release my focus on my job search and to see how being unemployed was a gift to me. She said this time in my life wasn't about me looking or not looking for a job; it was about me learning to get what I was supposed to get from not having a job. It wasn't about working, versus not working. It wasn't about money, versus no money. It was about lessons. When Melissa first said, "I'm not telling you not to look, I am telling you to learn the lessons," I couldn't see it. I think it was months later when I reconnected with an old childhood friend who said, "Maybe it is really about your son in his senior year." My ah-ha light bulb came on. It was clear it wasn't about me at all. It's about the fact he's leaving in a year, and this is my time with him. Our time was not when he was three, and I wished so badly I could be home—it is now. I followed my new insight by asking him, "Do you care if I am or am not home? Does it do anything for you?" And he said, "You know, I don't need you to be home, but when I get home in the afternoon, it is really nice when you are here, Mom. Don't you like it when you come home, and somebody is home?" So now a few times a week he comes home for lunch, and on those days I prepare something really fun to eat. It is creating a memory for us; creating a positive time, which will be part of our memories forever.

Knowing there are no coincidences has changed my life. I am now much more aware of the opportunities, messages, and lessons coming to me every day. I feel empowered to make choices. I release being confined by how I want things to turn out, and instead look for the gift and lesson coming to me. You have all kinds of ways to live in your perfect life. I feel very fortunate and grateful to be closer to living in mine.

LESSONS LEARNED

• The State of Gray is the foundation of Awareness and is achieved by turning off, releasing, and surrendering.

• Having the courage to look for and correct the root problem provides lasting change.

• The individual facets of mind, body, and spirit must be in balance for joy.

• Our word choice affects how we experience life.

• Our physical symptoms alert us to where we need to make changes in our life.

• Awareness of how our unique body works empowers us.

• Soul food is a great way to relieve stress.

DAILY HABIT OPTIONS

• Enter the *State of Gray* (see pp. 66) at least fifteen minutes every day by turning off, releasing, and surrendering.

• Use the *Association Awareness Query* (see pp. 67), *Word Choice Query* (see pp. 68), *Take Your Own Advice* (see pp. 68), *Body Talk* (see pp. 69), and/or *Food Journal* (see pp. 69) to learn more about the effects your beliefs, thoughts, words, actions, and reactions have on your everyday life.

THE STATE OF GRAY
Here are some ways to enter the State of Gray.

• Meditation or Guided Imagery: Unplug for fifteen minutes each and every day, turn off outside stimulation, and find the peaceful, quiet core within. Turn off all outside stimulation, including phones, email, radio, and televisions. Ban other people from the room. Focus on your breath and relaxing your muscles. Clear your mind of all thought. If thoughts come up, banish them from your mind until you are finished. Ask them to wait in the other room while you unplug. Try listening to a guided imagery or meditation CD to help you learn how. You can download a Heart Meditation recording at www.DownloadTypeMe.com.

• Yoga, Tai Chi, Chi Gong, or other body, breathing, mind practices: Find a teacher or DVD focusing on the mental as well as physical aspects of these practices.

• Drive-Time Quiet Time: Start by driving without the radio on and without making phone calls. Just experience the act of driving.

• Repetition: Engage in any repetitive, simple physical actions like walking, running, knitting, playing solitaire, etc. While you are doing the activity, breathe in through your nose, and then exhale from your mouth with a sound. If your mind wanders, place your attention on the action of your muscles, and nothing else.

• Breathing techniques: Conscious breathing brings us into the moment. One way is to breathe in through your nose, hold the breath, and release it through your mouth. Research different techniques, and see what works for you.

• Be creative: Pull out the crayons and markers and get lost in coloring. Relax and have fun.

• Chant: Find a meaningful phrase. It helps to find or translate the phrase into a language you don't know so your left brain does not gain control by focusing on the words. I personally use "Om gum shreem maha, lak shmee yea shaha," which is intended to remove obstacles in one's life.

• Mindfulness Reminders: Use intrusions as reminders to be mindful. For instance, every time a phone rings or you receive an email or text message, use it as a reminder to be present and in the moment like you are in the State of Gray. Before eating, take a deep breath and connect to the quiet of the State of Gray.

ASSOCIATION AWARENESS QUERY

Use the Association Awareness Query to grow your awareness of your unconscious behaviors, feelings, and thoughts. Start by identifying the less than desirable Actions or behaviors you are exhibiting. Next, note the Circumstance in which they occur. Then, identify how your Emotions and Body are when you are in this Action. Finally, notice any Thoughts you have about yourself, others, or the situation. Going through this sequence, you can begin to find correlations between your mind, body, spirit, and experience.

• Note any Actions (behaviors you exhibit) you would like to change.

• Note the Circumstance (situation) when you notice such action occurring.

• Note the Feeling you have right before, during, or after the action you would like to change.

• Note how your Body feels, and any specific physical symptoms you experience.

• Identify the Thought (limiting belief) you have that is causing the feeling.

You can also use these questions, starting with any undesirable emotional feelings or how your body feels. Next, uncover the Action, Circumstance, and Thought corresponding to your less-than-desirable experience.

WORD CHOICE QUERY

A variation of the Association Awareness Query is the Word Choice Query. This exercise helps us realize how our word choices create our experiences and affect our interactions with others.

• What was said, and the word choice used.
• Note the situation or context of your words, who was there, and what was occurring.
• Note how you felt during and after your words.
• Note how others reacted to what you said.

TAKE YOUR OWN ADVICE

Those around us often mirror the lessons we most need to hear and learn. It is often very easy to give the advice to others, advice we need to be aware of and incorporate for ourselves. Record advice you give to others. Now look through the situations and the advice to bring awareness of those things you could work on or improve for yourself.

• Gave advice to _____.
• Advice given was _____.
• Lesson for me was _____.

BODY TALK

As we have learned, our physical body and emotional wellbeing are interrelated. Being aware of how your body speaks to you allows you to uncover where you are out of balance. Use the prompts below to record possible emotional or situational causes of your physical illnesses. Over time, you can develop a good picture of the messages your body is sending you.

• Describe the physical ailment or discomfort you are experiencing.

• Note the current event you are engaged in or have just participated in.

• How are you feeling emotionally?

• Rate your current stress level (10 being most stressed).

• If you tried to change the state with medication or homeopathic remedy, how well did it work?

You can also use these prompts, starting with how you are feeling or the current event, and by answering the other questions, uncover how your body physically reacts. Either way, you are learning your body's unique language.

FOOD JOURNAL

Use the Food Journal prompts to uncover your own unique biological system, and what feeds it best. This diary can also be used to investigate not only food, but also to uncover the correlation between undesirable habits, like cigarettes and nail biting, and their emotional or situational cause.

• Write down what is going on before you eat (normal meal time, or when you choose to snack).

- Note the feeling you have right before you consume the food.
- Note if you were actually hungry before choosing to eat.
- Note what you consumed.
- Note how your body feels after consumption.

CHAPTER 4

Release the Baggage

Acceptance is not submission; it is acknowledgement of
the facts of the situation. Then deciding what you're
going to do about it.
— Kathleen Casey Theisen, Canadian politician

In Charles Dickens's *A Christmas Carol,* Ebenezer Scrooge's partner, Jacob Marley, wears the chain he forged in life. Marley said, "I wear the chain I forged in life . . . I made it link by link, and yard by yard; I girded it on of my own free will, and of my own free will I wore it." This is also true for our lack of forgiveness. When we don't forgive the driver for cutting us off, another link. When we don't forgive our parents for being human, it's another link. When we don't forgive our spouse for doing as much as they are capable of doing, it's another link. When we don't forgive ourselves for our past faults and choices, more links. Our chains become heavier and heavier. Unlike Jacob Marley, we wear our chains in our lifetime, not after death.

Every memory we hold of when we were wronged by others, a victim of circumstances, or ashamed of our own actions is a weight in our body and our mind. These memories of pain weigh us down. When chains keep us tied to the past, we're unable to experience the present. The chains make our expectations of future events negative and tainted. We are joyless, expecting only pain and hurt. We are bitter about what we have experienced, what has been done to us. Without forgiveness, we cannot release these heavy chains we carry around with us every day.

Sometimes we hold on to our pain because it makes us feel righteous. If we forgive someone for the pain they caused, we think we have let them off the hook. Sometimes we hold on to the pain because we want to protect ourselves. If we forget what happened, it will happen again. Sometimes we consciously or unconsciously refuse to forgive, in order to keep ourselves in the role of victim. We keep ourselves small, because we do not think we are capable of anything grand.

What if we could bypass forgiveness? What if in Acceptance we can find we have nothing to forgive?

- Acceptance is the act of tolerating without protest. It is not acquiescing, submitting, yielding, excusing, or approving.
- Acceptance is about how we experience an event. It is not about excusing others or the situation.
- Acceptance is the way we can release the emotional pain we have due to our judgment about others, their actions, or things we've had happen to us.
- Acceptance is a place of safety and security.
- Acceptance provides us with freedom.

REALITY IS RELATIVE

To learn Acceptance, we first need to learn no absolute truth exists, only perception. To do this, we are going to touch on the world of science to help us break through our ridged beliefs, allowing us the space to find Acceptance. A little article written in 1905 shattered some of the absolutes the scientific community assumed then. An unpretentious patent clerk, Albert Einstein, wrote a piece called "On the Electrodynamics of Moving Bodies." What he wrote revolutionized how we conceptualize time and space.

Everything is relative. Even though one single incident occurs, Einstein theorized, there is not one single truth about the incident. Depending on the location of the observer, the facts are different, and therefore truth or reality as we define it is also different. To give an example, say you are on the ground watching me float overhead in a hot air balloon. In the balloon, I am bouncing a shiny blue ball. To me, the ball is hitting the exact same spot on the floor each time it drops. To me, I see no movement or no distance traveled except for the distance from my hand to the bottom of the basket. To you looking from land, the ball is traveling across the sky. As the balloon moves, so does the basket, and so does the ball. From my perspective, only vertical movement exists, from your perspective, the ball is also traveling horizontally. Therefore, we have two different realities for the same incident.

Let's continue the hot air balloon scenario and say something the speed of light flies by me while I am in the basket. Again, think of me as an observer in the air and you on the ground. From my point of view, the object only traveled the distance of my basket. From your point of view, it traveled the distance of the basket plus or minus whatever distance the basket traveled. The speed of light, thought by the scientific community to be a fixed 186,282 miles (299,792 kilometers) per second, is in reality only true from the perspective of earth. The speed of light changes, depending from where it is measured. This experiment showed time is now also in the hands of the observer. The perspective and vantage point we each have affects how we see time and space. Not a single reality, but multiple realities exist depending on where we are situated.

To understand there is no absolute truth, only perception, we must know how our senses work. The physical world we experience is processed by our senses, and fed to our minds to create what we perceive. What our senses receive is not what we think of as reality. For instance, what our eyes receive are not images of a tree with apples, but they receive waves of energy. Each brown branch, green leaf, and red apple is actually a grouping of vibrating atoms and molecules emitting energy, which our eyes receive and pass to our visual cortex for processing. Our visual cortex interprets this energetic data into the colors and shapes of what we "see."

Dr. Jill Bolte Taylor, author of *My Stroke of Insight*, has a beautiful explanation of this process. Here is just a snippet: "A visual image is built by our brain's ability to package groups of pixels [vibrating atoms and molecules] together in the form of edges. Different edges with different orientations—vertical, horizontal, and oblique, combine to form complex images. Different groups of cells in our brain add depth, color and motion to what we see."[7]

What we visually see is not reality. What we see is our interpretation of what vibrating atoms form. Sight is relative. This holds true for our other senses as well. We are not "feeling" cashmere. Our brains are interpreting the energetic vibrations of the atoms comprising the fabric cashmere. The world we see and experience is actually our personal interpretation of vibrational waves.

If we put this together, recent quantum physics experiments show reality is based on the perspective of the observer, and what is observed is an interpretation of energetic vibrations. So, what is real? Moving out of the scientific world and into your personal life, these findings are incredibly powerful. Reality is based on the observer. What I perceive as reality is different than what you perceive. Our own unique point of observation, and how our brain processes what we observe, affects how we see and experience life. Acceptance begins when we can release the belief there is only one way, only one choice, and begin to recognize and accept life unrestricted.

Hillary took her husband's word as gospel. What he said was the truth. She did not trust her own beliefs and perceptions. Even something as simple as deciding how to cut grass—Hillary's husband would tell her she was not doing it correctly, and she would believe him. Her husband would tell her she was wrong, and she should do it the way he said was so obviously right. She thought her way could be valid, but didn't speak up because she believed her husband knew "reality" better than she could. She assumed only one way is right, and her husband knew what it was. She did not trust her own heart and mind. In always accepting her husband's thoughts as facts, she felt stuck. Hillary tried to accept what he said was the only absolute truth; however, no matter how hard she tried, she could not see it. When her perception did not match his, she felt guilty or frustrated. She wanted to "fit in" and be accepted by her husband. As we explored how our perceptions color our reality, or as Hillary said, "Every story has at least two sides," she could begin to accept herself, her life, and her experience as valid. She stopped denying herself and her feelings. She stopped trying to force herself to accept her husband's version of truth.

When we are stuck in our rigid thinking, trying to force those things around us to fit into what we currently know or want to believe, we can often miss the truth of the situation. Part of Acceptance is recognizing we are not all-knowing. It is admitting we have some beliefs and judgments we may need to adjust. Sometimes it is because what we know is no longer relevant because technology, the environment, and other aspects of our lives are constantly evolving. Sometimes it is because the life we know does not match the experience of others' lives. Acceptance is openness. It is allowing the truth of every situation to reveal itself.

- Acceptance is meeting every circumstance and individual with an open mind. It is releasing our preconceptions and expectations.
- Acceptance is greeting each situation with a blank slate. It is experiencing each moment as it is without the stories of our past.
- Acceptance is seeing what is there, not trying to force the situation into what we expect or want to see.
- Acceptance is openness without judgment.
- Acceptance releases our personal agenda. It allows us to see others and situations as they are, not how we wish or expect them to be.
- Acceptance is seeing the world objectively, not through our perceptions, beliefs, or past experiences.

The principle of Acceptance empowers us to release black-and-white "facts," and instead relax into Acceptance of "reality" from our own Type-Me personal perspective. What do you assert is reality? What do you believe, like time and space, is a rigid, immovable fact, but maybe isn't? Which of these hard-and-fast, black-and-white thoughts are causing you pain, unhappiness, and a sense of powerlessness?

THERE ARE ABSOLUTELY NO ABSOLUTES
Multiple realities, not one single reality, exist because multiple individuals, perspectives, experiences, and circumstances exist. The experience of life in Uganda is true and does not negate the experience of life in Scotland. Each is true to a particular situation.

Neither is more right or better. They are both equally factual. The world and we are constantly changing and evolving, so truth is also not static. What was true for me at fourteen is not the same for me at forty, but both are true within a particular time and situation. Truth is variable based on the observer, time, location, and situation. One right answer with well-defined boundaries does not exist. An entire spectrum of possibilities is available to us. With over seven billion people on the earth, I am guessing we have at least as many different versions of the truth and what life is all about.

By acknowledging differences, we can begin to accept our unique Type Me self and those unique individuals around us with their own Type Me, because all of our truths can exist together and not exclude any other truth. If reality is based on our perspective, we have over seven billion realities—one for each person on the planet. No one reality is more right than the other. My view of reality is not negated by yours, and vice versa. My liking and enjoying rock-and-roll music does not negate your appreciation for country music. Those of us who attack another's beliefs and perspectives only cause pain and conflict. As long as the beliefs are not harming others, who cares? To each her own.

All too often, painful issues arise when we assume we have only one absolute truth. We expect others to act like us, think like us, be like us. We believe in one absolute, unmovable way of life. We expect others to have the same perspectives and values. We become angered when they act differently, believe differently, and do not value what we value. When I was first married, and the initial love-induced blindness began to fade, a host of differences came to light. For example, I like to have the living room table free from magazines, newspapers, and mail, while my husband tends to stack piles of paper. Although I love him dearly, this aggravated me to no end. Unlike what you may be thinking, the true issue was not our different habits. A couple can always learn how to live in the same space. If I brought the situation to his attention, he was more than willing to find a resolution. The true source of my pain was not the state of the table. My pain was because I *assumed* my husband and the entire universe viewed living room tables the way I did, and therefore I perceived the stacks of magazines as a purposeful attack on me.

My husband's true nature is to stack. This is his truth. It is what he does naturally. It is his version of reality. It is his Type Me. My pain was the expectation he should act differently from his true nature. What caused me pain was my assumption his goals for the living room should be exactly the same as mine. I assumed the way the living room table should be was an absolute to which everyone adheres. I expected and wanted him to act as I would. I expected him to be like me. As I assumed he thought like me, I perceived his stacking as a willful act of disrespect. I found relief when I accepted my husband as he is, and released my beliefs and interpretations about why he was acting as he was. When we release the idea our preferences, beliefs, and expectations are law, we can begin to accept others as they are, and find peace through compromise and understanding.

In working with my clients, eventually we come to a point where they are frustrated with how someone is acting. "They *should* be doing something different." "They *should* see the situation as I do." "They *shouldn't* be doing what they are doing." Much of our pain comes from expecting people to act other than how they are acting. If someone were truly willing and capable of acting differently, that person would be doing it. The truth is, they are not. And as we have learned, desiring other than the truth causes pain.

Just the other day I was teaching a class, and one of the participants was angry her uncle did not have the same sense of responsibility she did. As a very driven woman, Susan expected others to feel the same accountability, and therefore to take the same decisive actions she would. I had her imagine a car. It was easy to imagine this woman as the engine of the car, powerful, strong, and making things happen. But a car is more than just an engine. It needs a steering wheel, driver's seat, wheels, brakes, and a host of other parts to make it work properly. When we expect others to be like us, we stop the car from running properly. All parts have their own function and purpose. When we see how each part fits together to make the whole, we can find relief from expecting others to be different from their truth. Susan found relief as she thought of her uncle as the radio of the car. The radio makes driving more enjoyable, and would be missed by many if it were not there, but its function has nothing to do with the actual act of driving. Susan could now stop expecting her uncle to be an engine like her, and accept his role as radio.

Acknowledging others as they are provides a great release.

• Acceptance is the act of release. Acceptance is releasing our beliefs in absolute codes of conduct. We may personally prefer certain codes, but they may not be inherent to those around us. Expecting everyone is, and should be, like us only causes pain.

• Acceptance is only releasing our expectations and desires for them to act differently so we can receive the peace of seeing and being in the truth. It is a different matter how we react or act around those whose truth may have negative effects.

• Accepting others as they are can be easier when we can see and understand their role and purpose.

• Accepting others becomes more difficult when we see their truth, choices, or actions hurting others or themselves. It is important to note Acceptance does not mean approval. It simply means we recognize their truth.

- Acceptance does not mean we have to be a victim of their choices. We can still protect ourselves, and remove ourselves from harmful situations.

In Acceptance, "should" and "have to" do not exist. In Acceptance, we begin to understand the only restrictions we put on others are the ones we create. It is important to be aware not all groups of people have the same set of expected actions. Would the behavior expected on Wall Street be the same as the behavior expected by a tribe in the Amazon? Depending on where a person comes from, and where they are on their journey, their behavior, focus, and actions may not match our own. The frustration from expecting others to match our beliefs, and act accordingly, is a pain we can avoid.

IT'S NOT ME, IT'S **YOU**

Janice was angry at her co-worker. "Why does Hank always take credit for my work in meetings? Why does he talk over what I am saying? Why is he trying to ruin my career?" I stopped Janice in her story. When we tell our stories, we express what is happening to us. We are the protagonists of the story, and everything is filtered through our perception. Instead, I had Janice try to look from Hank's perspective. I asked her, "Why could Hank be acting as he is?" The truth is, Hank was not trying to do anything to Janice. Hank was frightened. He thought his job was in trouble, and he was grasping at any way he could to try to protect his job. Now, Janice and I agreed it was not the best choice for Hank to take credit for others' work, but once Janice understood it was not about her personally, she found relief. Janice could now address the true issue: Hank's fear of losing his job. Her feeling Hank was attacking her was a symptom, not the cause of the issue. The true cause was Hank's fear. It wasn't about her. It was about him.

When we stop focusing on our own experience, it opens us to see the issue from another's perspective, and perhaps find a truth we can address. Acceptance is also about seeing situations from the perspective of others involved, and not just from our perspective.

Most of us have heard the adage, "Don't assume because it makes an *ass* out of yo*u* and *me*." But do we realize the number and intensity of assumptions we are making throughout the day? "She was late for our meeting *because she disrespects me*." "He didn't finish his project on time *to undermine my authority*." "She never tells me what is going on *because she doesn't care about me*." Unless someone tells us directly his motivation for his behavior, we can never really know for sure. The result: our self-created assumed motivations can be a cause for further conflict and pain.

Ever notice when we are upset, we immediately blame someone else? "Why didn't he consider me?" "Why does she have to be so rude?" "Why is he always disrespecting me by being late?" It is so easy to find a reason to blame another party. They aren't doing X, or they always do Y to hurt me. But the truth is, their actions are not to blame for your pain and unhappiness—you are.

What someone else does or does not do is a fact, not a personal attack. Really. Even if somewhere in the other person's psyche they are trying to hurt you, you have to believe you are being hurt. You need to interpret their actions as vindictive. You are the one in control of judging the situation, and determining your experience of it. No one else. You choose to succumb to another's anger or attack. You can also choose to see past it, and to not add emotion to fact.

I have found two main motivations behind people's actions: self-preservation and inherent nature:

1) **Self-preservation** appears in many different forms. Self-preservation may be fear of not being accepted and loved. Self-preservation may be fear of security—financial, job position, or social. Self-preservation may also be the desire to have comfort and pleasure. Self-preservation often appears as defensiveness, attack, judgment, and pride. If we acknowledge his or her desire for self-preservation, we can see the individual as being frightened and insecure. This allows us to find compassion and acceptance.

2) The other motivation for action is simply one of **inherent nature**. We are punctual or time doesn't matter. We show love through gifts or through words. We are verbose or hardly talk. Remember, no one right or wrong way to be exists. The problem is when we believe someone *should* act in a certain way; it is usually in the way we act or would prefer them to act.

Take a moment the next time you feel someone is doing something to you. Find the facts of the situation. Filter out your assumptions and emotions. Look at the possible motivations behind the actions of others. See if you can't make the situation better just because of the way you perceive it, and by beginning to understand what might be going on with the other person to cause the situation.

YOUR UNIQUE TYPE ME

During my Corporate America years, one of the companies I worked for sent us to personality testing to help grow understanding and communication between associates. The test determined which of four personality types we were. Each of the personality types was represented by a different color. The test indicated I was an organizationally focused Green, but I was really attracted to the synthesizing, holistic, integrating, creative

Yellow. I felt in my heart I wanted to be and could be Yellow, but the executive trainer told me I was a through-and-through Green, and I just had to accept it. He was partially right. At the time, I was a deep Green and I needed to accept who I was. We cannot move forward until we accept where we are in the current moment. If we lie about the reality we are experiencing, it is difficult to change our reality.

But the executive trainer was wrong about who I truly was. I was acting as a Green, hiding in the safe, rigid, predictable, controlling world of Green (e.g., Type A). But my heart longed to be Yellow, creatively seeing the world in a different light, bringing thoughts and ideas together in new and groundbreaking ways. Once my heart could feel what it would be like to be Yellow, a fire began to grow inside me. As I began to trust in my truth, I could let loose of my Green ways and embrace the world of Yellow, finding peace, joy, happiness, and fulfillment. Now I have learned to embrace the tools of my Green ways without being ruled by them, and enjoy a healthy balance between Green and Yellow.

Stress relief is found not only through accepting others, but also from accepting yourself. This is done by uncovering and embracing your inherent gifts and essential genuine self, your unique Type Me. One way or another, every client who comes to me is struggling because they have not embraced their Type Me. Who they truly are is out of balance with who they think they need to be. They are trying to live by the rules their parents or authorities outlined. They are trying to succeed in a field that makes their skin crawl because they think they need the money. They are living a false life, trying to look and act like their peers, when their hearts desire something completely different. They put others' needs before theirs, and therefore never express or experience their own truth. They are off-track, stifling themselves, pushing down their dreams until their dreams are forgotten, living a bland, disappointing life, hiding in tasks and to-do's so they don't have to be alone with themselves and see how unhappy they are. They are too frozen in fear to even try to take a step toward their truth.

Back in high school I heard the Henry David Thoreau quote, "The mass of men lead lives of quiet desperation." At the time, it resonated with my teenage angst, but the quote has become more poignant as I moved through life. So many people, and I was one of them, lead lives of quiet desperation. They move through their day, going through the motions, and hoping for the one small, infrequent blip of happiness, or they hide their pain in addictions and distractions. Somewhere we as a society decided it was acceptable to be unfulfilled, and only a few of the lucky ones get to live the life of their heart's calling. I wholeheartedly disagree. We all have the right and the ability to live our personal Type Me.

My favorite stories about being authentic, and not being authentic, are about the same person, Michael Jordan. When Michael Jordan played basketball, he made it look easy. He seemed to fly through the air. Everything he did looked effortless. But did you know Michael tried his hand at baseball? He was awful. Not really, but in comparison to his basketball skills, he was maybe just average. So what was the difference?

Basketball is Michael's inherent Type Me. Basketball is his purpose, his heart's desire. He is physically built to play the game, and he is passionate about the game. On the other hand, baseball was chosen for Michael. Depending on the story you have heard, it was to honor his father's wishes, or it was penance for gambling, but either way, it was the result of outside forces bringing him to the game, not his own passion and desire to play it. Baseball did not please his soul. It was not what he was born to do. He was never going to be for baseball what he was for basketball. It was not his Type Me.

Many people experience pain from trying to be something different than their own unique Type Me. These people are:

• Holding themselves back because it is not proper, appropriate, or acceptable to be what their heart desires.

• Trying to do what society wants them to do—pleasing parents, spouses, and bosses. They do not believe they have the right to the life they personally desire.

• Trying to get by with good enough because they fear the risks it would take to try to achieve their dreams. Their fear of instability and poverty overpowers their dreams and purpose.

• Experiencing pain, stress, and unhappiness as the result of not acknowledging and accepting their personal Type Me.

For many of us, knowing and accepting our unique Type Me is a mystery we can't answer, and sometimes don't even want to explore. We fear if our Type Me is uncovered, we may learn the life we are in right now might not match where we are meant to be. It could mean changing jobs, locations, partners, cars, activities, clothes, or any other element of our lives. Embracing our authentic Type Me may mean a shift in friendships, and perhaps some rocky times with our families. Making major life changes can be scary, but making those changes can also lead you to an amazingly fulfilling life, which is unimaginable to you right now.

On a recent trip, I spoke to an eighty-five-year-old man who would not share his true heart's calling with me, but he spoke with sadness as he described an unfulfilling yet lucrative career in finance. Even after all he had been through in his life, he had terror in his eyes when I told him of others who took risks to live their dreams. To me, the stories of risking what is safe to experience your true heart's desire are uplifting. To him, it was an impossible and inconceivable task. It broke my heart to see the sadness in his eyes as he revisited his never-realized dream.

I am thrilled to be working with some college students who are willing to explore their Type Me. They are bravely pursuing their dreams, instead of following the path educators or their parents laid out for them. It is not only for the young. I have many older clients who are exploring new careers in their fifties, or looking at retirement as the time they are finally ready to embrace their Type Me. Whether it is a career, lifestyle, hobby, or way of life, many of my clients are now bravely embracing their own Type Me, releasing the bonds of stress and worry, and experiencing the joy their Type Me provides.

In her new book, *Thrive*, Arianna Huffington asks, "Have you ever noticed that when we die, our eulogies celebrate our lives very differently from the way society defines success?"[8] We spend our entire lives striving for success, money, titles, accomplishments, and societal definitions of beauty, yet we are remembered for how we *lived*. Being Type Me is about how we live based on our own unique definitions of success, purpose, and joy. Unfortunately for many of us, we have stifled living our purpose because of fear.

- We fear we will not be taken seriously if we pursue a career as an actor or musician.
- We fear we will never make a lot of money as a botanist or artist.
- We fear our family will not accept us if we become a police officer or veterinarian instead of joining the family business.
- We fear we will be discredited if we embrace our personal values instead of the current societal values of money and prestige.

When we are younger, our parents often try to protect us by pushing us into "safe" and "secure" careers and life choices. In doing so, they usually inadvertently keep us from exploring our own purpose and passions. Next, schools, universities, personality testing, and career aptitude tests try to categorize, label, and contain us into existing conventional norms. Finally, our peers and society present us with their definitions of success and happiness, which can become hindrances if they do not reflect our own values. Accepting our Type Me means reclaiming our unique purpose. If you are currently in a less than ideal job, you can download ten ways to make your current position better (www. DownloadTypeMe.com) as you begin to explore your Type Me.

Accepting ourselves does not only concern our jobs. Acceptance includes acceptance of your true Type Me. It is accepting what your heart calls you to do on and off the job. It is accepting your height, weight, hair color, and every physical feature. It is accepting the way you talk, walk, and eat. It is accepting what makes you laugh, and how you laugh. It is accepting what feeds your soul. It is accepting and loving your unique Type Me.

To accept our true selves, we need to shift our definition of success and happiness from those provided outside of us by our families, peers, and society to our own personal definition. This takes a lot of courage, but it is well worth the risk.

PERFECTLY IMPERFECT

Sophie didn't like her nose and wanted to have surgery to make it perfect. After we explored what she didn't like about her nose, we dug deeper to find out why those things were important. Sophie felt a need to be perfect, and she viewed the way her nose curved to the right as an imperfection. Whenever she spoke to someone, she thought they were staring at her nose and judging her poorly because of it, which made her feel "less than." We worked through her thoughts of being judged. How many people were truly judging her? If some people are judging her, why was she holding their opinions so highly? And most importantly, we talked about why she was judging herself. Why couldn't she feel comfortable in her own skin? Sophie thought she had to look perfect to receive love.

Many of us are like Sophie. We feel our bodies need to be perfect. We need to dress perfectly. We need to speak perfectly. We need to act perfectly. We need to complete each task perfectly. *The desire for perfection is usually wrapped around conditional love.* If we don't look and do everything perfectly, we feel we do not deserve to receive approval, affection, and love. Some of us even reject love given to us because we feel we did not achieve the self-created conditions to receive love. We can also fear imperfection because we are afraid of being judged or attacked.

Sophie and I explored why she tied her appearance to love. When she was growing up, she received the most attention from her parents and other adults related to her appearance. She created the belief the two were tied together. I had Sophie imagine she had a horrible accident and lost her nose completely. Would she be undeserving of love for the rest of her life? Logic told her this was untrue. Next, I had her imagine holding back love from her child because of the way she looked. She could not do it, and started to realize she was the one who had set up and held herself to those standards.

What is *perfect* anyway? Who determines the definition of perfect? When we realize perfection is based on *perception and choice*, we can move past our desire to meet any standard not feeling good to us. Standards are arbitrary. Why hold ourselves to them? Instead of believing we need to embrace our imperfections, we can be empowered by redefining what is perfect. Our unique Type Me is what is perfect, at least perfect for us. We do not need approval from others. We do not need to feel embarrassed by our uniqueness. We do not need to apologize for who we are naturally.

Imperfection is the new perfect. Accept yourself as human. Give yourself permission to be imperfect. True acceptance is accepting your full self, including your quirks, flaws, and things we may want to change. Being your Type Me takes the courage to accept those parts of us others may not like or approve. When you can step into your unique Type Me, you can find power you never knew you had because you are no longer hiding yourself.

JUST SAY NO

Once we begin to understand, accept, and embrace our Type Me, we need to make space for it in our lives. Look around you. What are things you have said yes to, things you have agreed to do, tasks you feel responsible for, that do not feel good to you? What holds you down in your life because it is not your own?

Type A's have a tendency to be caretakers and people pleasers. We accept or take on tasks because we want those people we love to be taken care of and happy. Type A's jump into projects because they feel they can do it best, before looking to see if it is their true responsibility, and more importantly, their pleasure, to do it. We also jump into what needs to be done because it fills our self-worth and sense of accomplishment. The result: we are overloaded with things to do, and we feel powerless or resistant to letting anything slide. We lose who we are, our Type Me, in all we do for the needs of others.

When I lived in a condominium, I attended the association board meetings. When they held elections, I ran for one of the open spots. I didn't really want to be on the board, but they needed the help, and I felt I should participate. Being on the board wore me down. I am a morning person, and the board met at night, and it involved many hours of work, and no pay. Although I could technically do the work, it brought me absolutely no pleasure. Once I realized it was a bad fit, I felt powerless to step down. How could I abandon the other board members? How could I abandon my duty? My husband and I talked through the idea of "duty." The truth was I was not responsible for the state of the condominium. Also, because I was so unhappy, I was executing my job poorly. In realizing I did not owe anything to the board, and also that staying in my position was actually keeping someone more interested and capable from taking over, I was able to release my self-imposed responsibility.

To reclaim our Type Me, we need to start saying no. This is often difficult for the Type A because we can see what can be done, and have a knee-jerk reaction to start doing it. Or we feel that refusing to do what we are asked to do makes us a bad person. However, every time we take on something that is not ours to do, we are hurting ourselves. Every project we take on that does not energize our Type Me drains us. Every time we do something we feel we "have" to do, we are filled with resentment. Every time we choose to do something that does not fit our Type Me, it takes us away from something that could fulfill us. In saying no, we are saying yes to our Type Me.

We are not the only ones hurt by taking on what is not ours. We may also hurt others by taking on what is their responsibility. Imagine you never taught your child to tie her own shoes. Every day you would lovingly tie her shoes. You want to take care of her, and you know you can tie shoes better than she can, so you take on the task. This act of love robs your child of learning, of learning how to take care of herself, and it robs her of self-respect. Sometimes giving to others minimizes them and their own power. Who are people in your life who are being hurt, rather than helped, by you stepping in?

Shifting responsibilities does not have to be all or nothing. Rebecca was the only relative of her aging uncle, and she felt responsible for his health and wellbeing. Every doctor's appointment she arrived early to take him. Every time he needed to go to the store, she drove him. Every issue he had, she jumped to resolve. Rebecca felt like a slave to her uncle's needs. However, she also felt like she was a bad person if she admitted his care was becoming too much.

Rebecca and I talked through the difference between duty and doing. Her duty, and really what was true to her Type Me, was her desire to help her uncle. *Doing* was the problem. It was just too much, and it took her away from what she wanted to do. She felt she did not have a life because she put her uncle's needs first. Together we problem solved how to reduce her involvement in the doing. She chose to take her uncle to the doctor because she wanted to be there for him, and for her own knowledge. For the other tasks weighing Rebecca down, we found a different way to get them done, just not by her. For instance, we found a service to drive him to the store when he wanted. Saying no does not have to be absolute. It may just mean saying no to the parts not feeding your Type Me.

Look at all the places you are currently involved. What is truly your responsibility? What do you enjoy doing? What feels like it is controlling your life? What is your duty? What is some "doing" you can release? What feeds your Type Me, and what takes you away from it?

AN EVEN EXCHANGE

When we take on everyone else's responsibilities, we become depleted. Besides saying no to what is not ours, we also need to learn to let in what we need. Type A's have a hard time receiving.

We are so focused on everyone else's needs, we hardly notice what we need. Part of learning our Type Me is getting back in touch with what our needs are. If we desire something, it is hard for us to define and ask for it, and God forbid, receive it. In doing so, we drain ourselves to the point of not being able to help anyone.

Much of why it is hard to receive is tied to *conditional love.* We don't allow ourselves to receive because we don't believe we deserve. No matter how much we work, and how much we give to others, we do not believe we are meant to receive even a portion of care in return. Sometimes we think if we do receive something, we will now owe the other person. Sometimes we simply are so busy we aren't aware of our needs. If our needs aren't scheduled like a dentist appointment, they aren't even acknowledged. Sometimes we are afraid of accepting help and support because it would show us to be weak, and not a superhuman Type A. Sometimes we are terrified of letting go of control, because we did not trust we would be taken care of if we don't do it ourselves.

I was all of the above. I had no idea what made me happy, but it didn't matter because I didn't have time to examine what was missing from my life. If anyone would try to help me, I would push them away, afraid I would lose my power, or I would reject their kind intentions because I didn't think I deserved care and concern. I was depleted and exhausted, but would never dream of asking for help. I remember even rejecting when someone would open a door for me. How dare he! I could open the door myself.

My loving husband tried to break down this tendency, and made some progress. But he could not make the change for me. The way to start receiving was for me to begin accepting. After fighting over my bag (and losing) with one of the employees at the retreat in Peru, I decided to allow myself to be taken care of while I was there. It wasn't easy asking for what I needed— and receiving it fully and openly. I had never acted this way before. I learned to identify what I needed, ask for it, and receive it without excuse, fear, or feeling I owed anyone. When I returned home, I strengthened this skill: learning what I need, having the courage to ask for it, and accepting it openly, and with gratitude. Receiving is anti-Type A. Type A's control and do. We make things happen. Receiving is seen as weakness. Receiving takes some shine off our Type A badge. The truth is we are empowered, energized, and supported by receiving. It is safe, okay, and normal to receive. Part of Acceptance is accepting we are human, with needs and desires to be fulfilled. We deserve to have our needs met.

Tabitha gave and gave and gave. She was awesome at taking care of her family, co-workers, and clients. What Tabitha was not good at was receiving. She always had some "yes, but" reason why she shouldn't receive. It all revolved around deserving. Together, we would explore all of the logical reasons she should receive unconditionally, and although she agreed with them, she would not allow herself to embrace receiving unconditionally. Next, we talked about her children. What was she modeling for them? She realized they were learning to deny themselves, and they are less than others. The desire to raise her children to be the best they could be became the impetus for Tabitha to begin to receive.

If receiving is still a difficult concept to embrace, think of it this way: taking care of our needs is extremely important, not only for us, but for those around us. If we reject help, assistance, support, and nourishment, we will become run down. If we are run down, we cannot help others. If you can't receive for your own wellbeing, do it for all those you care about and love.

THE GIFT OF ACCEPTANCE

Acceptance is a return to harmony with truth. This means an acceptance for how others acted in the past, or perhaps even what we did in the past. It also means accepting the truth of our current situation. In seeing clients struggling with being overweight, the first thing we work on is accepting one's own weight, to see the truth of it, dealing with the reality of the current situation. If we focused solely on the goal of losing weight, we are working outside of reality. Our ideal weight is a hope, a wish, an expectation. Our judgment is the situation should be different than it is. Once we can accept the truth of the current situation, we are *empowered to change it.*

When we pray for something to be different, we render ourselves powerless. Whether it is our weight, an illness, or our current work situation, if we focus on wanting the situation to be different, we are powerless to change it. Unfortunately, our society loves to spend time complaining about our woes, and how our boss, spouse, or fortunes should be different. To affect change, we need to accept the current situation as it is, not as we wish it would be. By seeing the truth, we are empowered to find solutions or fixes for what displeases us. The power of acceptance is by seeing the truth, we are empowered to find peace, and to make changes based on the reality of the situation. Acceptance allows us to explore our Alternatives, which we will discuss in the next chapter.

As we have seen, the act of releasing black-and-white views of time, space, and our perception leads to also releasing the black-and-white views of how we believe others should be, and how we believe we have to act and behave. Black-and-white absolutes lead to misunderstandings, restrictions, and pain. Acceptance of expansive, all-encompassing gray variations leads to joy and peace.

Acceptance is so much more than forgiveness. It is seeing the world, people, situations, and ourself objectively. It is releasing our beliefs and expectations to see and understand the truth as it really is. It is to understand we have multiple perceptions about life, and each is right for its own unique situation. It is staying true to our unique Type Me while respecting and honoring others' Type Me's. Accepting others, circumstances, unnecessary responsibilities, and our needs releases us from our stress, pain, and unhappiness.

CLIENT'S TYPE-ME STORY: ME IS SINGULAR

By Renee Renz

I initially came to Melissa to receive assistance for the business I was starting. I was looking for help with business planning, and to learn operations basics. What I received was guidance for not only my business, but for my life as well. Starting a business is a very challenging time. To balance company needs, while still taking care of personal and family requirements, involves an overwhelming amount of tasks, challenges, and time. The first lesson to really hit home was to stop splitting myself. To get everything done, and in the way I thought it *had* to be done, I wanted to replicate myself. I wanted to create a different persona for each different requirement. I wanted to know how to balance wearing so many different hats. Melissa had me reframe my goal. Trying to balance all the different hats I thought I had to wear was splitting me, breaking me apart, and causing stress. We instead focused on embracing only one hat: the hat of me. Different threads may run through it, different areas require my focus at different times, but only one hat—and only one me.

Once I centered in myself, I had more control over what was going on, and no longer felt pulled in different directions.

Knowing I had only one me, and knowing who I truly am, was also powerful for my business. Business becomes easy when you find *you*. A lot of things stopped me from being who I am. Besides various responsibilities pulling me in different directions, my beliefs and assumptions restricted what I thought I could do. These beliefs were so deep I thought they were fact. I took these beliefs from my parents, and from society as a whole. Unfortunately, our culture tends to restrict our creativity and self-awareness. Through the Habits of Awareness and Acceptance, I was brought out of bondage and found the real me. I was the butterfly coming out of the cocoon. I found my place in the world where I could truly be *me*. I got into the flow of being me, and once I found the flow of my personal passion and purpose, my business also began to flow.

Throughout the process, I was amazed at how issues in my home or in my relationships affected how I went about business. I remember coming to Melissa to discuss the services I wanted to offer my clients, but I started out by talking about some issues I was having with my family's responsiveness. What amazed me was how these little annoyances at home pointed to a larger issue for me to work on, which was affecting my business as well. It was all about me stepping into my power. I needed to set rules and boundaries. I needed to be an authority. I realized if I can't take the authoritative role at home, I can't do it outside of the home very well either.

At a conference I heard Dr. Frank Sovinsky, author of *The E-Myth Chiropractor*, say, "We don't break habits. We learn to disrupt them sooner." Melissa helped me disrupt my habits by bringing awareness to those things tripping me up and allowing me to handle them before they became a bigger problem.

Many of the issues affecting me came from my ancient family belief systems. Much of what we believe is set into stone by the time we turn four years old. Through conscious questioning and unconscious metaphor work, Melissa uncovered my belief in being the victim or the martyr. I had a history of giving up myself to make things easier. I would carry other people's pain and bear their burdens thinking I was helping them by being sympathetic, something I picked up from my mother. The result is I was weighed down by others' baggage, their needs, their desires, and their negative energy. Because of this I wasn't able to be the fullest me. I wasn't being present for myself, let alone others. Melissa explored different situations where I took this role. In seeing the situation from the others' point of view, I realized those I sacrificed for didn't even know I was bearing their burden. I began to learn how to notice others' needs and issues without taking them on personally. I separated myself from their energy. With this knowledge I was able to shed, once and for all, other people's burdens weighing me down unnecessarily. By bringing the beliefs to light that no longer serve me, questioning their validity, then choosing differently on a daily basis, I have been able to remove forever so much of what has held me back in the past. I learned how to find the true issue, face it, deal with it, and then erase it.

Learning this process from someone who does not judge has released me from judging myself—and others. When I stopped judging myself, accepted how I was acting, and realized I could choose to continue to act the same way or not, it gave me freedom, freedom from guilt and attack, to be able to choose better. I was able to step back and make choices from the perspective of what is best for me and my business. I no longer acted as I thought others wanted or expected me to. I found my own groove, knowing if things don't go as planned, I possess the ability and power to change them. In essence, I learned to step into my own greatness, and be comfortable doing so.

LESSONS LEARNED

- Reality is based on the observer and the observer's personal interpretation.
- Billions of ways to be exist, with no black-or-white absolutes.
- Trying to change another's Type Me only brings stress. Peace comes from accepting another's truth from his perspective.
- Happiness is found in accepting and embracing our own unique Type Me.
- To reclaim our Type Me, it is necessary to say no to anything not in alignment with it.
- Receiving is as important as giving.

DAILY HABIT OPTIONS

- Use *Twenty Questions* (see pp. 98) to evaluate difficult situations, uncover differing perspectives, and find acceptance of the situation and those involved.
- *Here Comes the Judge* (see pp. 100) brings your assumptions to light, revealing how your beliefs create stress in your life.
- The *Self-Talk* (see pp. 101) exercise will help you uncover the negative stories, limitations, and lack of acceptance you have for yourself.

TWENTY QUESTIONS

Twenty Questions can be used daily to help us expand our perspective to include other more objective observations, thus helping us embrace a new, more positive view of reality. Sometimes a good reality check can go a long way in helping us really understand the truth of the situation, and in that truth help us release our anxiety and stress. Re-framing our viewpoint can relieve stress by putting "reality" into a more joyful perspective. When you find yourself in an unpleasant situation, share with others you trust how you see the situation, and the outcomes you expect. Each day, use the Ask Yourself questions (12–20) to grow awareness of your assumptions and open your mind to other perspectives.

Ask Them:
1. Do they agree with your assessment of the situation?
2. Do they agree with your expected outcome?

Compare Views:
3. How do their views differ?
4. Why do their views differ?
5. How do you feel when you are in your perspective?
6. How do you feel when you look at things from others' perspectives?
7. Which way do you feel better?
8. If you weren't personally invested, would you still feel the same?
9. What is the "yes, but" keeping you from seeing and accepting another's viewpoint?
10. What is valid about your view?
11. What is valid about another's view?

Ask Yourself:
12. What assumption are you making about how you or others should act?

13. What assumptions are you making about what needs to be done?

14. What assumptions are you making about how things should be resolved?

15. Where do these assumptions come from?

16. What are three other possible viewpoints about this situation?

17. Is there a message for you in this experience?

18. What is the gift for you in this situation?

19. What can you learn from this?

20. What is the most important thing for you to focus on to find peace in this situation?

HERE COMES THE JUDGE

Here Comes the Judge helps us uncover our underlying black-and-white beliefs, those we apply to others and ourselves. Countless times a day we are not only noticing things about others, but also making judgments about them. To begin to know your judge, and how it is helping or hurting you, complete this exercise for a full week. Once you know your judge, be aware of the presumptions you are making each day. Question their validity and remove any presumptions causing you or others pain.

• Write the name of the individual to whom you are reacting.

• Note everything you physically notice about them, including their actions.

• Notice all the feelings arising from being with them.

• Uncover the belief you have about people, and how life should be lived, which is causing your feeling.

• Note if you only judge others by this belief, or if you also judge yourself, based on this belief.

For Example:
• Dan
  * He stacks papers, covering the living room table.
  * I feel disrespected.
  * Clean tables represent love and consideration.
  * I am judging both of us.

SELF-TALK

To begin on the path of self-acceptance, we must become aware of how we talk to ourselves. For a full week, be aware of your self-talk by answering the questions below. Once you have identified the self-talk stories, each day be aware of when they appear, and gently create a new story.

• Note what circumstances trigger your self-talk.
• What do you say to yourself about the situation?
• Is what you say supportive to your self-esteem and sense of self?
• How does the self-talk define the expectations you have for yourself?
• Does the self-talk limit you, and how?

CHAPTER 5

We Always Have Options

The most common way people give up their power is by thinking they don't have any.
— Alice Walker, African-American author and poet

Hopefully, you have already begun to notice the importance of Alternatives as we explored Awareness and Acceptance. In Awareness, we learned to tune in to our thoughts and beliefs, and began to recognize how they affect our actions and reactions. Next, in Acceptance, we learned how to accept and embrace our unique Type Me, and the Type Me's of others, as well as the multiple realities of every situation.

Alternatives arise from our ability to be in Awareness and Acceptance. Alternatives are where we learn how to create the life we want to experience. Alternatives are power.

- We can choose how we perceive, and how we interpret our perception.
- We can choose to see the world in constrictive black-and-white, or in a multitude of gray options.
- We can choose, and if we do not like the results, we can choose again.

Recognizing, accepting, and acting upon the knowledge that we always have Alternatives is the challenge. Living so long in a world of black-and-white has blinded us from our options. Living in a world based on fear and avoidance of pain has minimized our power to the point we feel we have *no control* over our lives. We so often feel we have no options.

Recently, I was speaking to a client, Lou, about how much he dislikes his job. Lou said he just had to put up with it because of the bad economy. He needs the money, and therefore, he had no other options except to stay where he is. I heartedly disagreed. We always have options. Lou has the option to find a new job or, more radically, to quit his current position, which he could do. It is possible. It would impact his current lifestyle, but it is an option. Quitting his job was not an option he wanted to choose, but just considering it as an option opened him up to seeing what other more acceptable options were available to him.

The key here is being empowered to see and truly consider every option available. Some options may be more palatable than others, but not seeing all the options keeps us trapped in the restrictive world of black-and-white. By looking at all the options, by playing in the field of gray, one is empowered to create a more peaceful, joyful, enjoyable life.

In this chapter, we will explore the power of Alternatives. Hold on to your hats because this chapter will open you up even further to a new understanding of the world you experience. In this chapter, you will release all reliance on victimhood, opening your mind to truly see the awesome power you have. You will step out of the comfortable cloak of powerlessness, and take the leap into your personal power. In this chapter, you will learn this power does exist, and how it is yours for the taking.

THE INFINITE PEACEFUL GRAY

Fear, worry, stress, sadness, and depression are usually the result of feeling constrained in some way. These unpleasant feelings are the result of assuming one is stuck between what makes one joyful, and what one believes he *has* to do. These feelings are the result of believing there is only one right way to be. These negative feelings come from expecting love, joy, success, safety, security, and happiness to be withheld if we do not act in a certain way.

The power of the Type-Me Habits breaks down these constraints, restrictive beliefs, and expectations of only conditional love to reveal how to live joyfully. Type-Me Habits release the confines of stressful limitation-based perception to bring about joy in every moment. It is a conscious choice to live with an open point of view, aware of various options in all situations. It is finding a peaceful shade of Type-Me gray in a world of black-and-white. It is living joyfully, no matter the external circumstances. The Type-Me Habits provide the freedom to always choose the absolute best, most joyful option.

Right now our society is very focused on black-and-white. You are a Republican or Democrat, a success or failure, urban or suburban, conformist or rebel, corporate or blue collar, beautiful or ugly, in or out, religious or atheist. It is hard to express one's thoughts without feeling forced to choose sides. In choosing sides, we are also forced to agree to the rigid dogma of that side. Wiggle room is not available. Having a view slightly different than a strict definition is seen as being inconsistent, waffling, or untruthful. Many of us feel lost, constrained, and limited, and *as if we have failed* because society has very little acceptance for the gray.

We often focus on the "black" of lack, limitation, sorrow, pain, anger, and injustice. When we live in this bleakness, it is hard to accept any joy. For example, when my father was diagnosed with cancer, it could have been easy to be in the black of fear, sadness, and impending loss. Through his ups and downs, I could have continually added to the pain I felt, making it grow and overtake my life. On the other hand, it would seem difficult to embrace a happy-go-lucky, Pollyanna, unrealistic, and perhaps disrespectful "white" overly positive attitude. Seeing the world only through rose-colored glasses can be a way to hide from the reality of life. Type-Me Habits are not about simply having a positive attitude instead of a negative one. Sometimes it is appropriate and necessary to be sad, but the degree and extent of such sadness, and how this sadness affects our life, is within our control. Using Type-Me Habits is not about hiding or lying about the realities of life by slapping on an unrealistic positive attitude. It is about uncovering the peaceful gray truth in every situation.

In the case of my father's illness I was sad, but instead of feeding my sadness with worries and victim thoughts, or blindly ignoring the truth of the situation with unrealistically positive thoughts, I found solace in a shade of gray. The gray I found came in the form of more quality time with my father in the last three years of his life than during the previous forty years. I accepted the truth of the situation, explored the alternative ways to be in the situation, and embraced the alternative that brought me more peace and contentment than either my black or white options did.

The digital palette has 256 shades of gray, and in reality, there are an infinite number of shades. Using the infinite number of shades between black and white frees us from being stifled between selecting only two less than desirable options. Releasing the bondage of black-and-white thinking, and opening oneself to the limitlessness of gray, is the root of empowerment. At almost every coaching session, I find myself using my hands to show the gray scale. My right hand represents the thought, action, responsibility, or condition found to be restrictive, confining, and dissatisfying. My left hand represents the absolute opposite, which appears to be unrealistic, impossible, or just as unsatisfactory as the right-hand option. I show my client the vast space between my hands, between their two assumed options, between their black and white, and ask them to move as far toward the left as they feel willing. Moving into the gray in-between provides them with relief. This visualization helps my clients to begin to be aware of and open to new, more satisfying options they never thought were possible.

Bill was experiencing a lot of stress from a demanding job. As his own boss, Bill had the power to determine how much he worked. However, he constantly took on more and more work. I asked Bill why he took on more than he could handle when he knew his enjoyment of life and his health were suffering. Through digging deeper and deeper into Bill's beliefs and assumptions, we uncovered a belief that if he was not working hard, Bill was letting others down, and therefore, he was a bad person. Although his extreme workload was causing great stress and unhappiness in his life, Bill felt he *had* to work long, hard hours. Anything less meant he was hurting others. By identifying the *black* of working hard but hurting himself, and the *white* of doing less work but hurting others, we were able to explore a more satisfying *gray* option. We found a lot of alternatives between working so hard it made him sick, and working so little he negatively affected his clients. This may seem quite logical from the outside, but when we are stuck in a black-and-white belief system, it can be very difficult to find the stress-free gray.

At times, it may be difficult to see the black-and-white constraints we have created for ourselves. Other times we feel the limitation of our thinking, but cannot find any other options. Still other times, we know what our better, happier gray Alternative is, but do not believe we have the power to choose it. When my clients are stuck in the black-and-white, I imagine them like a wind-up toy, the kind that walks into a wall yet continues to try to move forward. It walks and walks and walks, but doesn't get anywhere. Like my clients, the toy just continues to hit its head against the wall. This toy, like the client above, can only see one option available, pressing forward doing the same thing over and over again, receiving the same unsatisfactory results. To turn things around, it is assumed the absolute opposite choice needs to be taken—a choice that is not acceptable or desirable. But turning around does not have to mean choosing the absolute opposite. Turning around simply opens us up to more options than running into a brick wall.

Often the confinement of our black-and-white appears when we are afraid of being unloved, unaccepted, or shamed in some manner. Another client of mine, Betty, would be frantic during the holiday season. Betty would try to make everything absolutely perfect. The house needed to be sparkling clean, her children needed to be well behaved, the food needed to be exciting and tasty, and every inch of her house decorated as if Martha Stewart did it herself. Betty's *black was perfection*. This quest for perfection made her frantic, harried, and unhappy. She was terrified of being imperfect, of forgetting something or doing something "incorrectly." Without perfection, Betty felt she was the *white of failure*—unloved, unaccepted, and unworthy.

To open Betty to her alternatives, we first had to redefine her worth on something other than her perfectionist actions. We looked at others in her life. Did she withhold love from her children if they were not perfect? Did she excuse her husband and still love him even when he made mistakes? We looked to her birth family, who she was always trying to please. Did she hold them to the same standards she *thought* they were holding her?

Through deep exploration we determined the only person withholding love from her when she was less than, was her. Betty was stuck in black-and-white because she set the rules that either she was perfect or she was unloved. Once she realized she set the rules, she was ready to recreate rules allowing her the freedom to choose how she approached the holidays.

We investigated where she felt she needed to be perfect. For each instance, I had Betty question the necessity of perfection and the result that perfection had on her wellbeing. When Betty identified actions she felt obligated to do, but found no joy in, she allowed them to drop. She bought cookies instead of making them from scratch. She stopped staying up until four in the morning cleaning every inch of the house to ensure it was spotless. She used decorations from the year before instead of creating brand-new ones. With every risk, Betty inched into the gray, finding her fears were unfounded. She allowed herself to handle only the party preparations she truly enjoyed, while releasing any causing her stress. She learned how to be part of the party, not just a Stepford Wife hostess fulfilling others' needs. And for the first time in years, she enjoyed the celebration and her family.

Sometimes gray options do not appear as a single point between one set of black-and-white choices. We may not be able to describe the best option on a singular linear continuum. When I help people find their ideal careers, we do not simply choose between the black-and-white of a single career, like choosing between being an accountant or a lawyer. It is much more complex. At times like these, it can be helpful to break a situation down into multiple gray scales to find the ideal resolution. Think of an amplifier. It does not have only zero to ten for volume, but also has scales for treble, bass, gain, crossover, subsonic filter, slope, phase, bass boost, EQ, and a series of other audio options. Sometimes our perfect happiness is found at the intersection of all of these choices. For clients exploring new careers, I have them build many scales to review. Ideal career scales may include: office versus virtual, length of commute, company culture, opportunity for promotion, interaction with others, independence versus supervision, wages, benefits, and of course, all the different tasks and skills involved. Like setting an amplifier for your favorite song, uncovering the perfect position depends on finding the right setting for each of these career components.

Another way to really understand the breadth of options available, think of choices like a kaleidoscope. Each fleck of the kaleidoscope image is a specific point on a unique scale. A multitude of scales and a plethora of options on those scales are available all the time; it just depends on how you want to spin the kaleidoscope. If you are feeling stuck, turn your kaleidoscope to release the new ways and options always available to you. All scenarios exist in every moment; we just need to choose which option we want. If you are a procrastinator, or afraid to take the first step, know that your choice is not permanent. You can always choose again. We may think we want something now, but once we have it we may discover it is not what we expected. Okay, just spin the kaleidoscope and choose again.

Don't get caught up in trying to find the absolute very best choice. Don't be stifled by right and wrong. Just think of them as options. Sometimes we make choices that in the end show us what we don't want. Great! Now we know this piece of information, and we can choose differently next time. Perfect! Life is about choosing, experiencing, learning, and choosing again. Right and wrong do not exist. Good and bad do not exist. Only options exist. If we find the choice we made is not satisfactory, make another. No need to judge or label the choice as bad. Simply choose again. With each choice, we get closer and closer to a less stressful and more enjoyable life.

Our gray shades are always moving; like life they are fluid, evolving things. If you lock yourself into a shade of gray, this particular shade has now become your new black. Circumstances change. People change. The environment changes. It is important to remain fluid in your viewpoint as your life progresses. We are constantly changing and evolving. Our choice now may not be ideal later. Our choices in second grade are different than the ones in our second year of college, which are different than those in our second year of marriage. If you have achieved some goals, it is time to revise and create different ones. If the economy has changed, where you live and whom you live with has changed, or a million other variables have shifted in your life, it is important to ensure what you are focusing on and desiring is still true and valid for you in the ever-changing world. Keep turning your kaleidoscope to ensure you see all the possible variations at all times so you can choose what will make you joyful right now.

CHOOSE YOUR OWN EXPERIENCE

Our experience is based on our personal expectations, not on some set of outside rules and forces. We are in charge of what we perceive, and we are in charge of how we interpret what we perceive. By being actively aware of what we are expecting to perceive, we can change the realities of our own lives. We are not only interpreting reality, and choosing a positive or a negative interpretation, but by creating a positive expectation, we are creating a positive outcome.

A few years ago, I had pretty poor expectations for Thanksgiving. My cousin was hosting dinner downtown. My father didn't want to go because he thought his last round of chemotherapy to treat his cancer would make him tired. Since we are not going to my cousin's, I would miss spending the day with my great aunt and godmother, plus I was now in charge of planning a full meal for the parents. It also meant cleaning the house from top to bottom, which I despise. The thought of this Thanksgiving made me angry, sad, stressed, and really cranky. Imagine how my guests would experience me as I opened the door. Not very welcoming, huh? How do you think I would experience the event?

Luckily, I changed my expectations before anyone arrived. I thought about what a blessing it was to have my parents and mother-in-law over for Thanksgiving. They had all struggled with health issues over the past few years, so it was really wonderful to be able to share this special day together. As there would only be a few of us, we could really spend some quality time chatting and laughing. My godmother was in town for the week, so we would be able to extend the holidays by meeting up with her and my great aunt over the weekend. With those expectations in mind, how do you think I greeted my guests? I was much more welcoming with my new expectations, and I enjoyed the meal and our time together. In this scenario, I may not have changed anything but my own expectations, but the shifting of expectations also changed my experience of a situation.

Jolene, a teenage client of mine, was having a hard time getting along with her parents. She felt her parents did not understand or approve of her. Often when they were out together, they'd have conflicts. We talked about her expectations for an upcoming trip. When she told me about how she expected a fight, I could see her body tense up and her face become hard. I told her to imagine how she would ideally like the trip to transpire. Jolene did not envision a love fest, but she did express how they could get along and be together without personal attacks. Instead of expecting a fight on their trip, I told her to think about her desired experience. Before she got in the car, she was to pretend the trip went positively as she imagined. Every time she felt herself thinking her parents would attack her, she was to replay the image of what she desired. When we met at her next session, she was amazed at how easy it was to be with her parents. To me, it does not matter if she changed reality because of what she envisioned, or if focusing on what she desired softened her mood, leading to more positive reactions by her parents. To me what matters is her experience of life changed for the better due to her conscious choice.

Actively choosing our expectations is truly powerful. We can change our experience for the better by being aware of and adjusting our expectations to what we desire.

SIFTING THROUGH YOUR FILTER

My father's experience with cancer taught me much about patience with the unknown, acceptance of the truth no matter how painful, and gratitude for the smallest things in life. When my father developed a condition that put pressure on his brain, causing cognitive issues, he also showed the true power of our perception. During this time, his first symptom exhibited was a diminishing short-term memory. It started with forgetting small things like dates and locations, but escalated to not remembering what he ate five minutes before. He thought people visited who didn't, and forgot who did visit. This ailment branched into other areas besides memory.

One night I stayed in the hospital with him. We watched the show *Undercover Boss*, where CEOs pose as new employees to see firsthand the truth about how their company works. This particular episode was about Garden Fresh pre-packaged salads. My father started to wonder out loud what it would take to get a job at Garden Fresh. We chatted about this for a few minutes, but I realized this was not a hypothetical discussion. The nurse came in to take his vitals, and my father asked her how many bags of lettuce she packed a day. He truly thought she was a salad packer, not a nurse. He got angry when I tried to explain she was a nurse, and the job opportunity was just on a television show. He proceeded to ask me what position my brother and other family members landed, and wanted to know if they were all here, or at other parts of the company. My father thought he was in the show, and he was supposed to get a job. And things got even stranger. About a week later, we were watching a public television show about woodworking. For hours after the show, he complained about how strongly he could still smell the varnish they had used—on the television show. His ailment was now affecting his five senses, or the brain's interpretation of what these senses were experiencing. During both of these incidents, my father believed he was experiencing the real world.

It was very difficult to watch my father in this state, but I knew there was a lesson to be learned. I believe the lesson is our reality is created by what we perceive—and (unless we are not well) we can choose what we perceive. We choose what we focus on. We choose what we accept. We choose how we interpret different situations. Therefore, we are actively choosing our lives every day.

How many times have you gone to a party with a group of friends, and upon leaving, feel like you were at different events? One person had a great time reliving old times with old friends, one person was bored by the retelling of old stories, one person was disappointed they did not have enough dancing, and one person thought the food was phenomenal and worth the visit. Each of these individuals was at the same party—the same reality—but their focus and perception determined how they *experienced* that reality.

How we usually react to the information is the result of unconscious hard-wired responses, usually created early in childhood and colored by our family beliefs and early social environment. How we grew up, our experiences, our goals, our likes, and our dislikes all color how we see life around us. We choose how we interpret reality. Reality is relative to our personal filters.

Our experiences and beliefs determine where we put our focus. Our focus influences what slices of reality we experience. In 1975, psychologists Ulric Neisser and Robert Becklen conducted an experiment[9]. Test subjects were shown a video of people in white shirts throwing a ball back and forth with people in black shirts. The test subjects were asked to count how many times the ball was thrown. Next, the test subjects were just asked to *watch* a video. Again, people in white and black shirts were throwing a ball back and forth; then someone in a gorilla costume walked on screen, beat his chest, and left. It was the same video—really it was. However, the first time the test subjects missed the gorilla because they were so *focused* on the task at hand.

Don't believe it? Have you ever missed your turn because you are focused on your mobile phone conversation? You are still formulating the sales numbers for tomorrow's presentation, and you don't really listen to your child talk about school? So often we are focused on a single task, we shut out everything else, all other stimuli, all other thoughts. We are completely engrossed by what we want to complete. This tunnel vision can be terrific in order to finish our task, but it can also keep us from seeing and experiencing everything else. Years later, psychologists Arien Mack and Irvin Rock termed this phenomenon as *inattentional blindness.*

The reason behind this apparent blindness is our reticular activating system (RAS). Every day we receive tons of information. We are inundated with sounds from people, machines and nature, air temperature and the feel of wind on our faces, people and things to look at, the feel of our clothes on our bodies, the smell from lunch or a wet dog, not to mention all of the conversations, advertisements, and texts coming at us every second.

We literally receive four hundred million bits of information per second, but our brains can only process two thousand of them. Our brain cannot receive and make sense of all this data. We are not able to process and act upon all of this information, and therefore, the RAS filters it for us. The RAS sorts through and only delivers to our conscious minds the information on which we choose to focus.

My husband loves 1950s cars. On a busy highway, they just jump out at him. I'm not so interested. So if we drive around town together, unless he points them out, I will not see any 1950s cars, where he will see them all. Did he make 1950s cars appear? No, he has just trained his brain to actively bring them to his consciousness. If our teeny little brains tried to process and consciously make sense of every single piece of data we receive every second, we would probably implode. Therefore, our efficient and systematic brains automatically filter what information is received, processed, and retained. This is how my husband sees all those 1950s cars on the road. He filters *in* things he enjoys, like antique cars, while at the same time he is filtering *out* things he deems unimportant, like the billboard for The Container Store. RAS helps us receive only the data we want. It does not mean the other information does not exist. The billboard still exists, even if my husband doesn't notice it. Many things happen at every moment; what we focus on becomes our reality. For example, while I am writing this paragraph, I can switch my vision back and forth to either clearly see the text of the Microsoft Word document I am typing or see my image reflected by the computer screen. Both of these things are occurring at the same time. I consciously and unconsciously choose to see what I see from all the Alternatives available to me.

In the image above, do you see a young lady or an old woman? They are both in the same image. The old woman is facing to the left with a very pronounced nose and chin, yet if you switch your focus, you can see the profile of a young girl with a delicate nose wearing a necklace. Depending on which element of the image you first see, what someone tells you is in the illustration, or some other personal filter will dictate which woman you see. Our perception is affected by our knowledge and experience.

When you take your first sip of wine, you taste it and decide if you like its flavor, basing it on juices or alcoholic drinks you have had in the past. After an expert educates you about how different bouquets affect your olfactory senses, you experience the flavor of oak versus tannins and all of the other intricacies of wines, your next sip of wine will be a very different and richer experience. It is the same glass of wine, but the perception and experience of the observer are very different, and therefore, the results are different.

Sometimes not having had experience with something, or not having knowledge about it, will keep us from seeing it. When the explorer ships reached the shores of the Americas, the natives thought the sailors were superhuman. They thought the explorers sailed the seas using just the longboats they used to get from the tall ships to shore. The natives made this assumption because they had never seen a tall ship before, and had no comprehension of what these ships were. Therefore, their minds could not comprehend what they saw floating on the horizon were boats. It was not until the local medicine man was able to comprehend what he was seeing was a tall ship that others could also see these vessels.

It is like when we first learn a new language. At first *biblioteca* may mean nothing to us, but once we understand it means 'library' in Spanish, we can make the correlation in our minds. We cannot comprehend and perceive its meaning before our first day of Spanish class. We can't comprehend what we can't imagine, haven't experienced personally, or can't relate to in someone else's experience. For example, for the longest time it was believed humans were limited to how fast they could run a mile. All of our empirical data corroborated this fact. In 1954, Englishman Roger Bannister ran a four-minute mile, previously believed to have been impossible. He had broken through the assumption we all took as fact. Six weeks after this impossible feat happened, Australian John Landy also ran a four-minute mile. Once the impossible became a perceived possibility, others followed suit.

Once our RAS filters have become ingrained, it becomes our basis for black-and-white thinking. "I have to take a promotion under an awful manager, or I'll be fired and become a bag lady." "I have to go into accounting or my parents wasted their money on my education." "If I stand up for my work, I am being egocentric, so I will just have to let someone else take credit for it." When we think either in black or white, we become stifled. We feel forced to choose from two undesirable options, but we have to remember we also choose the options. We don't have to choose solely from the black-and-white options of our limited experience, focus, and belief system. Remember, we have available an infinite number of gray shades, and also an infinite number of Alternatives. By adjusting our filters, we can choose from among an infinite number of Alternatives available. Doing so can open up our thinking.

Take, for example, thinking that if you stand up for your work, it makes you egocentric. A lot of space exists between not taking credit and thinking you are a goddess to be worshiped. Open up your filter, look on the continuum, and find where you feel most comfortable. Where is a healthy and supportive space to be? How far can you take yourself out of victimhood and into self-respect? Becoming aware of and adjusting our filters gives us a whole array of new options and allows us to find the best personal choice for each of us.

WRITE YOUR STORY

- How do you perceive reality?
- How are you choosing to live your life?
- Do you focus on the good, or are you always looking at what is lacking?
- Do you share stories of heartbreak or joy?
- Do you acknowledge your small wins or focus only on the next challenge?
- Do you look forward to the future with hope, or are you resigned to a bleak future?

Through the years, we trained our reticular activating system (RAS) to receive only certain information.

- What have you trained your brain to receive?

- Do you focus on what is going into or coming out of your checking account?
- Do you remember the one nasty thing your sibling said to you, or the decades of good times the two of you had together?
- When you get a flat tire, do you start pouting and say, "Why does this always happen to me?" or do you thank your lucky stars you have a towing service through your insurance?

Over the years we have all had experiences in life, some better than others. By mirroring the adults around us, we began to learn (e.g., teach our minds) what elements of an event to focus on, and how to interpret it. As we grow up, we probably surround ourselves with people who have similar reticular activating system (RAS) filters, and therefore similar views of the world and how it works, further reinforcing our programming.

Sometimes this is a terrific thing. We may look at the world positively with hope and promise. We surround ourselves with those who see the universe as amiable and supportive. Sometimes, however, we choose the negative or off-balance viewpoint of our parents, so they will accept and take care of us. Or we grow up in a difficult household situation, and learn the coping mechanisms to help us through our youth, but hold us back when we are older. Or we hang around with a group at school that has an unhelpful worldview we take on as our own. Wherever we picked up pessimistic, victimhood, self-sabotaging, or hindering viewpoints by the time we reach adulthood, they are pretty well wired. Our brain's software is uniquely programmed to unconsciously choose how we perceive events, and how we make judgments and assumptions about those events. Because all of this programming is in the background, we believe what we are experiencing in the form of pain, heartbreak, indignity, exclusion, or anger is reality. But all of those things are not truth. They are our perception of reality, not the reality itself.

Remember my story about Thanksgiving, and how the facts were the same, but my experience of the day shifted greatly, depending on how I interpreted the situation? We do this every day with all of the situations we face. We hardly ever look at the cold, hard facts on their own without adding in our assumptions, judgments, and perceptions of the events. The truth is, we give events their meaning. A ring is just a piece of metal, but through a ceremony, it becomes the symbol of unity between a couple. In the same way, we place meaning on all of the events in our life. If we find a parking space, we are lucky or fortunate. If we are cut off in traffic, the other driver is a jerk who ruined our day. We create a painful or pleasurable experience by interpreting a set of facts and drawing conclusions about them. In this way, we are choosing, consciously or unconsciously, the amount of stress and pain that is in our life.

Yes, we can experience true pain. Grief, sorrow, and sadness can be true and honest pain. However, the amount of time we have these emotions, or the extent of the suffering we experience because of them, may not be true. According to brain expert Dr. Jill Bolte Taylor, sensory preceptors send signals to our brains, and upon receipt, our brain experiences real emotions for only a matter of ninety seconds.[10] If your emotion lingers longer, a story or judgment about the emotion is making it linger. Emotions infused with judgment and self-chosen negative connotations cause us pain. We create the dirty pain[11] in our lives. We consciously or unconsciously tell the pain to stay around. We wallow in the negativity, the pain, and the heartbreak for days, weeks, months, or years. On the other hand, true pain can be experienced, acknowledged, and then released all in a matter of moments. For some time after my father died, I would occasionally experience sadness when I was reminded of him or the times we shared. If I left it alone, a bittersweet sadness would wash over me, and quickly be released. If instead I added on to the story about how I didn't do enough for him, didn't say what I needed to or how much I miss him, the sadness would linger and grow.

We cannot control the situations we face. We are going to get laid off, break off a romance, or lose a loved one. Those real situations will occur, but we have complete control over how we interpret these situations. We cannot control the facts, but we can choose how we experience those facts. For example, here's a fact: you have one hundred dollars in your savings account. Your perception may be that you *only* have one hundred dollars *left* in your savings account. Your word choice paints a picture of lack and fear. Instead, you can choose to celebrate the idea after paying all your bills, you *still* have one hundred dollars in your account. Yes, this is the glass half-full or half-empty game, which some can see as simply choosing to be a Pollyanna optimist or a realistic pessimist, but it is so much more. The perception we choose to make also determines how we experience the situation. Having one hundred dollars does not create a feeling. How we interpret what the one hundred dollars means creates an experience. I am not asking you to be unrealistic about the situation. I am asking you to choose how you want to experience a certain situation. I want you to choose the perceptions that can help you feel your best.

This does not mean you can sit around eating bonbons instead of finding ways to pay your mortgage. Actions and experience are two different things. Actions are how we move about in this physical world. I need to be actively typing these words to have them appear on the page. I must take action. Actions are facts. I am standing, sitting, or reclining. Experiences are based on perception. The experience I have is based on how I want to, consciously or unconsciously, evaluate the action. For instance, a fact is you are lying on the couch. But your experience is quite different if you define this to mean you are a slacker, versus to mean you are receiving some much-deserved downtime. Peace is found through choosing the most pleasant experience we can by consciously choosing the most fulfilling perception of events. The ability to see Alternatives is not simply the act of positive thinking, and it's not about being overly optimistic. The ability to see Alternatives is being empowered to make the best choice available to you at all times.

When I was young, I loved to read the book series called *Choose Your Own Adventures*. These books were about the Wild West, outer space, dragons, or mysteries. The first few pages gave the premise for the book. For instance, in *The Third Planet from Altair*, Captain Bud Stanton, Professor Henry Pickens, and Dr. Nera Vivaldi head toward the third planet from Altair to investigate alien signals being detected from there. After a few pages of exposition, the reader is given a choice: if you want to land on the planet, go to page four; if you want to turn back, go to page ten. After you choose, the story continues for a few pages until another decision page appears. Sometimes the decisions you made would progress the story positively. But sometimes it would result in death or another less than desirable outcome.

During my father's illness, I caught myself in my own choose-your-own-adventure story, and I wasn't making the best choices. My actions didn't lead my adventure astray, but my words did. The simple question, "What's new with you?" would be posed. If I want to say something positive about my business, go to page four. If I choose to bring up my father's illness, go to page six. The story would continue on page six. "My goodness," my friends would say, "I am so sorry to hear about your dad." If I want to say, "Thanks, he's in good spirits," go to page eight. If I choose to say, "Us too, we're really worried," go to page ten. I did notice how my choice at every juncture led me closer and closer and deeper and deeper into negativity, until my focus was solely on the bad—because bad news was what I shared.

I also began to notice how others' reactions tainted how my adventure continued. If they were supportive and positive, I could rebound into seeing the current situation as just part of my life. But if they, meaning well, wanted to focus on the negative what if's, talk details about what could go wrong, and emphasize how this must be hard for me, then I would delve deeper and deeper into my how-bad-things-are story, which is a hard tailspin to stop. Our culture thrives on negativity, disaster, and fear. It is much easier to fall into such a mantra than one of optimism and hope.

I challenge you today to write your own adventure. Look at every juncture of your life.

- What do you choose to say, do, or believe?
- What result occurs because of the choice you made?
- Are you creating an adventure that ends in riches and joy?
- Or are you leading yourself down the path to defeat and negativity?
- What choice will you make?

Consciously be aware of the story you are creating, and re-write the parts that are harmful or unsupportive of you. Look at those things causing you stress, heartbreak, and pain. What is a true, honest fact, and what can you rewrite to be more helpful, motivating, and supportive? You can control what to experience by actively creating the story of your life, just as you want it, and with each conscious choice, you are reprogramming your subconscious.

REPROGRAM

Due to all the unconscious programming in our minds, trying to find available Alternatives can be difficult. Luckily, you don't have to keep any beliefs or perceptions that don't serve you. You can change your outlook, even if it seems to be hardwired in you. The medical field has commonly accepted the idea the brain is plastic or changeable. Back in the day, they thought certain parts of our brains were responsible for certain things, and it was all set at birth. However, scientists and medical doctors started to notice when people lost their sight later in life, the old visual receptors of the brain switched over and aided other senses. Or they saw that when the portion of the brain handling hearing was damaged, other portions of the brain stepped up and took over the hearing processing. We learned our brains are not stuck in one setting, but are continually changing and evolving. These changes are not only on an individual basis, but can be seen en masse; as new experiences and behaviors were added to our culture over time, changes to the brain occurred. Dr. Jill Bolte Taylor asserts, "The development of language, for example, has altered our brains' anatomical structure and cellular networks."[12]

We can consciously change the wiring of our minds. We have the power to not only choose how we perceive, act, and react, but we can also go into our gray matter to delete old programs not working for us, and wire together new programs that serve us better. As Dr. Stephen Larsen, psychotherapist and author of *The Fundamentalist Mind: How Polarized Thinking Imperils Us All*, says, when we can release the old programs "Sometimes a tremendous amount of energy is released. People start new projects, their creativity opens up, and they don't feel stuck anymore. A healthy brain is always a flexible brain, just as a healthy body is a flexible body."[13] Releasing old programming leads to having more power to affect how you experience life.

The good news is what we have currently programmed in our minds is not permanent. Due to the plasticity of the brain, we can actively retrain it, and create new and healthier unconscious perceptions and actions. The bad news is our fears may be what are holding us back from adopting a new way of thinking. Identify anything you perceive you will lose in letting go of the old. Will you lose friends, security, or the life you have known? Change can be difficult, but if the change sends us toward what is better for us, it is worth the transition. Most of our fears of change are negative, restrictive beliefs and can be removed by rewriting our stories, but a few special beliefs come up in regards to change. They are: 1) change is permanent, 2) change negatively affects others, and 3) change will negatively affect the future.

1) Change is permanent. If I choose to make a change in my life, I need to live with it for the rest of my life. Wrong. We are in constant flux. What we choose today we may not choose for tomorrow, which is okay. Choose again. Yes, you can choose again. You can change as frequently or infrequently as you like. No choice is ever permanent.

2) Change negatively affects others. As I like to believe, no one is going to actively choose to do something to intentionally physically hurt another. Our fear is about how another will perceive ways our actions are affecting them. This is not something we can control. No matter how pure and honorable our intentions, someone else may consciously or unconsciously view it as an attack, slight, or loss. This is their perception. We cannot be responsible for it. Just as we need to be responsible for how we perceive our lives, others need to be responsible for how they experience their lives. Just as we are empowered to change our experience, so are they.

3) Change will negatively affect the future. We hold onto a pain of the past, and assume the future will be the same. Or we fear now about a future we can't control. Are you where you thought you would be five years ago? If not, how can you believe you can predict exactly how things will be five years from now? All you can know is this moment. Don't give your mind the painful incidents of the past, or the fearful images of the future, to experience. Focus on this moment, and if real pain exists in this moment, choose a new Alternative.

Samantha was holding herself back. She was afraid to be fully her Type Me because she thought her friends and family would reject her. I asked her what was better: to have friends who like you because you constrain yourself into their way of being, or to have friends who truly see and approve of you for who you are? She chose the latter, but really didn't know how to make the change. Samantha didn't know what her new life would look like, so she didn't know what major change she had to make to get there. The answer is not one major change, but a series of minor changes to lead her to what she wants. I told Samantha to focus on freedom and joy, as this is the experience she wanted. She was also to be aware throughout her day if what she was doing, who she was with, or how she was acting made her feel freedom or joy. If not, she was to make one small choice to move her closer to the feeling she desired. When we think we need to make sweeping changes to our lives, we can become stifled and terrified. An easier way, and one to help us reprogram our minds, is making small daily choices.

Reprogramming our brains takes conscious and continuous choices. By growing our Awareness, we now have a platform to uncover Alternatives. We can notice how we believe, think, speak, and act, and also notice the effect these have on our lives for the positive or negative. In the moment, or as soon as possible afterward, we can choose to continue doing as we are, or shift our beliefs, thoughts, words, and actions just enough to make our experience better. Every time we do this, we are sending new programs to our minds. Eventually, these better choices will become unconscious. It is like riding a bicycle. When we are first learning, we need to be consciously aware of how we are pedaling, steering, and balancing. With time and practice, these movements become unconscious, and we can ride a bike without thinking about each action we need to make. The same goes for reprogramming our minds. Start by making conscious choices about what you want to experience in each and every moment. With time and persistence, this new way of being will become a habit, and will happen unconsciously.

As a single footstep will not make a path on the earth, so a single thought will not make a new pathway in the mind. To make a deep physical path, we need to walk the same steps again and again. To make a deep mental path, we must think over and over the kind of thoughts we wish to dominate our lives. Going through this process every day begins running new grooves in our minds until eventually we have a new worldview. This is why this book teaches Daily Type-Me Habits.

Remember your current programming is based on years or decades of thought deeply ingrained into your subconscious. It will take effort and time to rewire your unconscious. This does not mean if you are thirty years old, it will take you another thirty years to reprogram, but it does mean you need to be vigilant. You need to be actively aware every day of the stories you are writing. A time will come when it looks like you have completely rewired your brain. But things change, like you are in a different job, with a new partner, learning new hobbies, or networking with new groups. As your environment, relationships, and circumstances change, old issues you have not yet addressed, or have not addressed in regards to your current condition/situation, may come to the surface. I was doing really well with my personal re-programming. I had rewritten a lot of the programs no longer serving me, and I was doing very well, flying blissfully through life on autopilot. However, in the last few months of my father's life, the stress I and my family were experiencing sent us all back to behaviors from forty years earlier, dredging up feelings, fears, and bad habits we earlier had regulated to the sidelines. It took Awareness of falling back into old habits, and actively choosing new, better perceptions from all the Alternatives available to me, to help dig myself out again.

Be gentle with yourself. Just as athletes and performers have to practice and strengthen their muscles, you will also have to strengthen your mental muscles. Give yourself time to build up new wiring, and cut yourself some slack if you need to regroup and refocus after being thrown into a new situation.

A powerful tool available to help you reprogram your brain is the Daily Type-Me Habit of the State of Gray. If we are not taking the time to center and calm our minds, we cannot have Awareness, and without Awareness, we cannot uncover and choose from the Alternatives available to us. If we are heavily focused on the litany of beliefs our left brain spouts at us, it is difficult to choose something new. Relax. Quiet your mind. In doing so you will be able to reprogram your mind, and regain the innocence, connectedness, freedom, and energy of a child.

Sometimes all of this cognitive effort doesn't work. Perhaps your perceptions are too ingrained; perhaps your current habits keep your mind from being clear; perhaps an old emotional wound won't heal with logic; perhaps some factor is just way too scary and your conscious mind will not allow it to the surface. At these times, you may want to look at your whole self. Are there things in your diet you can change to help quiet your mind? Do you need to release food or alcohol addictions before you can do any mental work? Or do you need to look into some emotion or energetic healing before you can address things cognitively? Remember, you have many aspects, and just as I did through my Peruvian experience, you may need to address each of those areas to find the relief you desire.

Becoming Aware of our current beliefs, actions, and habits, Accepting the current situation and releasing our fears, then choosing from the available Alternatives all takes a lot of guts and determination. But it is worth it. Really it is. Take your time going through the process. Don't try to force things to change any faster than feels comfortable. The key to reprogramming your brain is to take the first baby step, which will give you the courage to take the next. Don't look at the distance you need to travel, just focus on what is next to accomplish. As they say, the journey of a million miles starts with one step.

CLIENT'S TYPE-ME STORY: TAKING CARE OF ME

By Tamera Harrison

Over the past ten years I had flown back and forth from the Midwest to the West Coast to take care of my brother and mother, who both had cancer. It was stressful to see them with this disease. I took on caring for my sister for a couple of years when she came for a visit, and while with me, my sister ended up with a serious case of Crohn's disease. I thought I was doing good things for others: being there for people I cared for, supporting my family, my daughters, and supporting someone I thought I was in love with and married to. But eventually it was too much. It all caught up to me, and my body just said, "This is enough. You can't continue to put yourself on hold. You can't put everything you want and need to the side. You are going to have to, at some point, address yourself."

My wake-up call started when I had to have hip replacement surgery. The feeling of being helpless was so terrifying, I was literally begging the doctor to not do the surgery. I could hardly walk, but I was so terrified of being an invalid. I started noticing the stress when I had to be dependent on other people. Two years later my body said, "Ok, I guess you haven't learned your lesson. Well, you know what? You are going to be dependent again because you have breast cancer now. Let's see where that is going to take you." But I was slow to learn. All the time of my hip surgery and my own cancer, I was still taking care of my family members.

As I started working with Melissa, she opened up some doors for me. I began to learn to deal with the cancer, to deal with my feelings about my mate—the one person who was supposed to be there for me when I needed him—and to begin allowing other people to be there for me.

I began to understand my perceptions were sometimes not reality. My perceptions of being self-reliant, "No, I don't need anyone to take care of me," were melting away. One tool I used was reframing how I was going to perceive a situation. I would state my perception of a situation as "I can't lay down and just be lazy because I have so much to do." Melissa would say, "How else could you say the same thing in a more positive way?" I would reframe my thought to "It's okay for me to lie down and rest. It's okay to let things go." Melissa would say, "How else can you say it?" She wanted me to do it three different ways. I struggled because I felt like I just wanted to get it done. I wanted to rush through the mental exercise, and not think too hard about it. When I took the time to do this exercise, it helped me release stress and pain. I still use this tool almost every day. When I am faced with a difficulty, I think about my perception of the situation. How am I processing this? What would happen if I processed the situation differently? If I changed my thoughts, how would this situation change? This is the approach I now take, and it has helped me become a much happier, outgoing person. I can now find the most positive way to look at a situation.

One of the hardest things was to allow myself to truly express my feelings about a situation or an individual. It was hard to recognize and acknowledge when people upset me. Melissa made me look at things from the other side of me, the side of me who was exhausted from allowing others to do things that hurt me. She helped me get past my rose-colored glasses, and helped me safely access the angry part of myself so I could come back to the safe space in between where I could honestly express my feelings. It was very difficult. Through a series of baby steps, she helped me learn *I do have value, I do have worth.* I could see the truth about what was happening with my marriage—and some of my other relationships. I finally learned to say no. Enough is enough. No more. I was very scared because making the necessary changes in my life was not the best thing financially. But I was able to pull myself together, and I now knew I had people I could depend on. I am now in a much stronger place with all of my relationships, and I trust myself more.

Before I often just wanted to escape the pain of a bad situation. Now, instead of trying to get out of the situation immediately, I try to look at it differently. Even though it may be painful, I have the courage to face it. I try to see how this difficult situation is taking me to a better place, even if what I am experiencing right now is not ideal. That is the acceptance part. I am not escaping or ignoring my life. I am taking my life back. It has taken a long time, and I still struggle sometimes, but I have the tools now to help bring the true issues to the forefront. For the most part, I utilize those tools.

I now try to stay as open as I can be. I pay attention, and learn from what is happening. I look at what journey this situation is taking me on. I ask myself, "What I am learning from this?" With my recent car accident, I immediately thought, "Oh yeah, okay dummy, so you are thinking about where you want to be instead of being focused on the moment. You are trying to please other people by being on time for a meeting, instead of taking care of yourself by driving carefully." My reoccurrence of breast cancer was more difficult to identify. It was in part about having my mom take care of me. I was very emotional during, and I think the emotion of losing a breast was more than I had anticipated. My mother wasn't always the most empathetic person when I was emotional. She'd kind of pooh-pooh it, almost as if I was being unreasonable. I really appreciate the fact she was here to help me. She would cook and take care of me—the more physical side of things. She has difficulty handling the emotional side.

At first I was angry because I wasn't able to express how I was feeling, but I allowed myself to go there. I didn't let my mother stop me from expressing how I felt. Being able to do this helped me turn a corner with her. It helped me embrace the fact I am going to express how I feel, which I am doing more now. I am dating someone and I am expressing my feelings more with him. It is sometimes painful for people when I express my true feelings and emotions. It is hard for some people to accept, but I feel better in expressing them, no matter how they are received.

The last ten years have probably taken me toward finally being able to be authentic. I can now allow myself to just be who

I am. I can allow others to care for me, and I am putting my needs above the needs of others.

LESSONS LEARNED

- Stress is the result of limitations. Freedom and empowerment are the results of being open to Alternatives.
- We create our experiences of reality by what and how we choose to perceive.
- All Alternatives are available to us at all times. The Alternatives we perceive are based on what we filter through our reticular activating system (RAS).
- We can consciously choose our own story, and therefore our experience.
- Our brains are plastic, allowing us to change our mental programming through consistently and consciously choosing what is best for us.

DAILY HABIT OPTIONS

- Use *Expectations* (see pp. 133) to begin to understand and revise your unconscious programming.
- *Caught in the Act* (see pp. 135) will help you make new choices in the moment, or as close as possible.
- *Releasing Misperception* (see pp. 137) and *Prove It* (see pp. 138) will help you remove the blocks you might have to finding and accepting new alternatives.
- *Creating a Gray Scale* (see pp. 138) is a way to visualize all the Alternatives available so you can make the best choices.

EXPECTATIONS
Think of an upcoming difficult situation. This could be seeing

a challenging family member, confronting your boss, or going to your high school reunion. Whatever the situation, make it one you are not looking forward to, and perhaps even dreading.

Situation:

Write down your expectations for the event.

- I expect to see _____.
- I expect to hear others say _____.
- I expect to say _____.
- I expect to feel _____.
- I expect to think _____.
- I am afraid _____.

Now, think of how you would prefer to experience this situation. Create a new expectation for this event.

- I expect to see _____.
- I expect to hear others say_____.
- I expect to say _____.
- I expect to feel _____.
- I expect to think _____.
- I hope _____.

Read over your revised scenario at least twice before the event. After the event, write down everything you noticed.

- My attitude going into the event:
- How I acted:
- How others acted:
- How I reacted:
- How the event when overall:

• How the event transpired in relation to my expectations:

You can download (www.DownloadTypeMe.com) a copy of this powerful tool so you can always have it on hand to use.

CAUGHT IN THE ACT

Over-generalizations, absolutes, premonitions, and labeling discussed in Awareness not only can add pain to our experience, but they also further wire our brain circuits to expect a specific experience in the future. To stop or reverse these beliefs, we now need to catch ourselves using these word choices and make better choices in the moment. This can be tough. First, we may not be able to catch ourselves in the moment. Be patient. If you catch yourself a day later, fine. Think about what you could have said differently. Try to catch yourself closer and closer to the actual moment. Do this until you can be aware of your word choice before any words leave your mouth, so you can actively make better choices. As you begin to remove black-and-white (Always, Never), absolute (Have To, Should), and premonition (Almost, Could Have) language, you will begin to see the true reality of situations, and will begin to choose more soothing, positive, and helpful interpretations of what is going on.

A great way to break the cycle of previous programming is to incorporate pattern interruptions. These are tools you can use to take yourself out of the heat of the moment so you can make different choices. Pattern interruptions can also be stops throughout the day to give you time to reflect and be aware of what has happened, in order to give you the momentum for making new decisions in the future.

One pattern interrupter tool is *breathing*. Instead of launching into the story of your morning commute, take a deep breath and ask yourself what story you can tell to create a positive start for your day. Taking a deep breath helps to stifle the knee-jerk reactions and normal habits we all have, giving you space to make a new conscious choice.

Another pattern interruption tool is to *find points throughout the day*, at either specific times or using specific events like meals or drive time, to remind you to stop and check in. When you stop, ask yourself if you are choosing healthy, beneficial thoughts and actions, or if you are falling into old unproductive habits. Don't berate yourself if you are sliding downhill. Instead, congratulate yourself for becoming Aware, and then concentrate on choosing better Alternatives.

Sometimes our negative beliefs are really solidly hardwired and appear to be fact. One can usually recognize these by the feeling of constriction and hopelessness they provide. These negative beliefs serve to restrict and stop us. They keep us from pursuing our dreams, and worse, they pose as being a hard-fast reality, which cannot be removed. But are they truly reality, or are they just our perception? To break through these negative, limiting beliefs, search for the truth of the matter by releasing your black-and-white emotional reaction.

Byron Katie, author of *Loving What Is,* and queen of dissecting and dissolving limiting beliefs, shares a sequence in her book to help individuals remove the beliefs that are blocking them and causing pain. I find her first step to be incredibly powerful. Just ask yourself, "Is that true?" As I say to my clients, "Is your belief absolutely, 100 percent, provable-in-court true?" The answer is usually no.

Our fear of moving forward and taking responsibility for our lives and actions creates the perception these obstacles are real and true. We think if they are true, we are powerless victims who can do nothing to change our situation. Releasing yourself from the perception of limitation allows you to see the situation as it truly is. It opens up choices that were not there in limitation. It helps you to move past fear into empowerment.

RELEASING MISPERCEPTION

This exercise is designed to help you accept a new reality. Answer the following questions about something you want to reprogram in your mind.

It is hard to believe/accept:

Write three reasons why this statement is false.

1)
2)
3)

Write three examples of how this statement could be true.

1)
2)
3)

Imagine you believed the statement was true.

• What would you visually *see* in your life that would prove to you that you believed the statement was true?

• What would you hear others say about you if you believed the statement was true?

• What would you say about yourself if you believed the statement was true?

- Write down any negative consequences that may occur if you believed the statement was true.

Repeat the statement you have a hard time believing at least once a day to yourself (out loud or silently) for at least a week. Review the examples of how the statement could be true, and what you would experience in your life if you believed the statement was true. Update what you wrote to reflect any new thoughts you may have.

PROVE IT

Break through the power of the belief by remembering at least three times when the stifling belief was not true, or three times when the preferred belief *was* true. Again, we get what we focus on. If we tell ourselves again and again we are too old to go back to school, it becomes a fact. If instead we come up with a list of three people we know, or know of, who went back to school and graduated at older ages, we can shatter this restrictive belief.

Belief:
- Was not true.
- Was not true.
- Was not true.

Opposite of Belief:
- Was true.
- Was true.
- Was true.

CREATING A GRAY SCALE

Another way to break out of the all-or-nothing, black-and-white restrictive thinking is to find the shade of gray Alternative between those two points that can be as true to us, and also more motivating. For example, let's say you feel trapped at your job. You thought is, "I have to stay here or my family will starve." We could probably wipe this one out by asking if the statement is 100 percent true, but let's pretend we are still having trouble shaking it loose. What if we find a new statement that is just a little more comfortable, yet just as true for us, perhaps, "I have to have an income or my family will starve"? Just making the small shift from needing a paycheck from a specific company to just acknowledging you need positive money flow, opens up a world of gray Alternatives. It opens up the possibility of finding another job, and it frees us from the feeling of being trapped and enslaved. It is empowering.

CHAPTER 6

Walk the Talk

The most difficult thing is the decision to act, the rest is merely
tenacity. The fears are paper tigers. You can do anything you decide
to do. You can act to change and control your life;
and the procedure, the process is its own reward.
— Amelia Earhart, American aviation pioneer

The Habits of Awareness, Acceptance, and Alternatives are all
centered on cognitive thought, and all center around internal
work. The final habit, Action, is where the rubber meets the
road. This is where all the incredible internal work you have
been doing is made manifest in your actions and words. This is
where you use all you have learned to make tangible changes in
your life. Action is where you make manifest everything you have
learned, every moment of the day.

Counselors, psychologists, coaches, and other wellness practitioners are terrific at creating momentary positive experiences.
You attend a seminar, workshop, or a weekend retreat where you
learn new skills and ways of being. As you receive new information during the event you feel better, powerful, and joyful. But
the day after the event you are back to old unhelpful habits. This
was exactly what happened to me when I returned from Peru. I
had learned and experienced so much during my time with the

shaman. But when I returned to my day-to-day life, bit by bit my old actions, thoughts, beliefs, fears, and stress also returned. Like so many people, I became caught up with the hustle and bustle of modern life. The ten days living differently in Peru were no match to a lifetime of my Western life. I had learned new concepts but had not instilled new habits, and it was all too easy to fall back into the old behaviors, which had caused my poor health in the first place.

Instead of seeing how my old habits were the cause of my pain, I thought the healing with the shaman didn't work and searched for another cure. I searched for a program, process, or guru to help me find, once and for all, the happiness I desired. The truth is, no one perfect system or piece of knowledge will provide long-lasting relief from stress. The dirty little secret to self-improvement, according to neuropsychologist Dr. Rick Hanson, is that workshops, books, and counselors are good at creating positive experiences, but bad at making them long lasting.[14] This is where Action and you come in.

Type-Me Daily Habits are designed to help you not only have a great experience in the moment, but to create permanent change in the deepest part of your brain—the brain now mired in stress, fear, worry, and anxiety. The Type-Me Habits are designed to help you be more open, joyful, and aware of opportunities. To make lasting changes requires consciousness, diligence, and repetition. In this chapter, we will explore active ways to create lasting stress reduction.

A CONSTANT STATE OF PANIC

Again and again I would have clients who understood the concepts I presented, and would use them often. They would find days, weeks, and even months of joy and peace—until they experienced a life-changing event. Maybe a family member died, or they went through a divorce, or they had financial trouble. Immediately all the Type-Me knowledge they had was out the window, and they were acting out of their old habits. They mentally knew their behavior was not the best choice, yet they were acting unconsciously. They knew there was another way, but felt powerless or unable to choose it. I did extensive researching to find out why. Why did an individual, who cognitively knows better, end up making poor choices? I finally found the answer with the help of Natalie.

Natalie was a client perpetually stuck in a mire of anxiety, fear, and worry. Every occurrence in her life was a possibility for disaster. Every car trip became the possibility for an accident. The postman was not bringing letters, only bills. Her fears were not limited to what may happen in the future. Her anxiety-colored glasses also clouded events in both the past and present. Everything in her life had been a disaster. Every incident was interpreted to be negative. Even in the present moment, she could only see the bad. As a result, Natalie was depressed, bitter, and very unhappy. Yet she clung to her negative views like a security blanket.

Natalie was constantly attracted to and stuck in negativity. I would try to help her break free, but was frustrated by her natural tendency to jump back in and wallow around in the bad. Why did it take a conscious effort to release negative emotions? The answer is the age-old fight-or-flight response. Our physical body wants to survive; therefore, it is ever vigilantly seeking out things likely to hurt us. Natalie was stuck in fear because her fight-or-flight system was controlling how she experienced life.

To learn how all of this works, let's explore the brain's limbic system. This is the part of the brain that plays a major role in how we perceive and experience reality. *The limbic system* is comprised of the spinal cord, amygdala, cingulate gyrus, and thalamus. This system is commonly referred to as the reptilian brain because it is evolutionarily older than the cerebral cortex on the surface of our brain. The limbic brain is our survival brain. As we receive information through our senses, the data first goes to the amygdala, the fight-or-flight decision center in the limbic system, to be checked for danger. Teamed up with the amygdala is the cingulate gyrus. Since we don't want any delays in reacting to danger, this little guy creates a storehouse of automatic responses, depending on the sensory input. "Car is trying to merge, slow up." "Boss is coming, look busy." This is especially helpful if a tiger is coming at us. If we sit around debating the best course of action, we may become his lunch. Our limbic system activates our muscles so we start running away, sometimes even before we consciously realize the danger.

These automatic, pre-programmed responses can be very helpful, but they can get out of control. Often these habituated responses can lead to compulsive and obsessive behavior, irrationality, aggression, and an inability to release old pain. We can feel stuck in a thought or behavior, making our cognitive thinking cloudy and less rational. Also, the amygdala has the tendency to react to imagined danger with the same intensity as if it was real. "Oh no, a snake." Heartbeat increase. Leg muscles jump to safety. . . . "Oh, wait, it was just a stick." The amygdala is our source of fear, which is a terrific tool when we are in real danger, but it can become over-stimulated by imagined fears and worries to the point it can stifle the frontal lobe's logical thinking. When we are overcome with daily stressors, our minds are clouded in confusion and anxiety, overtaking our ability to problem solve.

Unfortunately, the limbic system's focus on fear has a high price in our modern age. Our instinctual responses to fear not only apply to running from a tiger, but also to many daily innocuous aspects of our life. Fight-or-flight kicks in when we are running late for work, worrying about our 401K, or having to talk with an annoying neighbor. Our minds are not able to separate between real and perceived fear. Watching violence on the evening news, in movies, or in video games sends our bodies into the same physical response as if we were actually participating in those life-or-death situations. Obviously we do not need our biological fight-or-flight reaction for these types of imagined threats, yet our bodies react as if the threat is real.

When our fight-or-flight reaction kicks in, it sends out signals to turn on high those parts of the body that will physically help us out of bodily danger. Our heart rate and cortisol levels increase to pump up our muscles' ability to react, while systems nonessential to survival, like digestion, reproduction, and immune, are turned off to conserve power. As producers of news programs, movies, and games have figured out, we also get an unconscious adrenaline rush when our fight-or-flight kicks in. Because of this, today our media is filled with horror, negativity, and disaster. We now live in a society constantly on an elevated threat-level alert from real and imaginary dangers. Because these threats are constant, we never turn off our body's reaction. Have you ever seen two ducks fight? Once they are finished, they will flutter their wings and basically turn off the fight-or-flight switch, releasing any residual tension. As humans are now moving from one stress trigger to the next, we do not have time to switch off. Without such a release, our bodies begin to experience deepened and extended stress levels, keeping important daily function systems turned off. The result is issues with reproduction, digestion, and illness because we are not feeding our essential systems.

All of this was reflected in the physical issues I experienced pre-Peru. I was on constant high alert fighting non-survival fears. I was worried about my job performance, deadlines, corporate politics, and lack of equality in the workplace. I was listening to the news, which was filled with fears of war, disaster, and poisons leeching out of plastic water bottles. The result: my body shut down daily functions like digestion and reproduction so it could be ready for battle. This translated to the high cortisol levels, and the host of issues I had with my body's normal daily functions. Plus, turning off my immune system gave me no power to fight the illnesses and the pains I was experiencing. Thus, the medication and treatments did not help me because they were focused on the symptoms I was experiencing, but not the core cause. It wasn't until I gained control of the signals my brain was sending to my body, and I could release the elevated stress levels, that I finally found relief from my pain.

Fortunately, everything has a balance. The anterior cingulate cortex (ACC) is the counterbalance to the knee-jerk reactions of the amygdala and cingulate gyrus. As neuropsychologist and best-selling author Dr. Rick Hanson states in his book, *Buddha's Brain: The Practical Neuroscience of Happiness*, the ACC "is a kind of a workspace where your brain gathers information to solve problems and make decisions."[15] Think of this as your computer desktop. Other programs might be running in the background or waiting in the wings to be activated and utilized, but your focus lies in the ACC. This is the area of self-control. Once the ACC has fully matured, somewhere around our third to sixth birthdays, we have active awareness and conscious ability to affect our thoughts and behaviors. The ACC is important because it can slow down or suppress the fears in the amygdala. To create a less stress-focused limbic system, we need to strengthen the ACC, make new choices, and focus on gratitude.

• **Strengthen the ACC.** The ACC needs to be strengthened, and the irrational reactions of the amygdala reduced. The State of Gray is the primary way to strengthen the ACC. Science has shown how meditation and other relaxation practices can increase the power and function of the ACC. A daily practice of the State of Gray provides you with a firm foundation to retrain the limbic system.

• **Make New Choices.** When we are unconscious, we are leaving our limbic system in charge, and allowing it to freak out about every possible and imaginable danger. Through Awareness, we can sort through the truth of the situation, determine what is real and what is imagined, and use our Alternatives to make new choices about how we perceive the situation.

• **Focus on Gratitude.** The final step is to switch one's focus from worry and fear to gratitude. Many spiritual and religious practices center around gratitude for a happier life. However, gratitude has been shown to have scientific value as well. Focusing on gratitude pulls power from our amygdala and moves it to our ACC. The more we focus on fear and worry, the more the amygdala is fed. The more we focus on gratitude, the more we strengthen our ACC.

THE POWER OF GIA

GIA stands for *gratitude, intention,* and *affirmation,* three overlapping and very powerful tools. Making gratitude, intention, and affirmation statements are the way you define how you see the world, and how you desire to experience it. GIA is the way to *create* your day. GIA is also a powerful tool for controlling our limbic system.

Gratitude

Gratitude is the opposite of anxiety. Gratitude is the act of enjoying and embracing life, whereas anxiety is the act of fearing and rejecting life. Being grateful is not just a religious or positive psychology tool, but it actually affects our brain's functioning. Our society has trained us to look for and focus on fear—fear of threats to our safety, fear of lack and not having enough, fear of not being loved. Fear is like a four-year-old feeling loss because she wants the toy her brother is playing with, when she is surrounded by fifty of her own toys. Gratitude is recognizing the other fifty toys. Focusing on lack and fear traps us in our limbic system of survival. The conscious act of gratitude releases us from a state of survival and allows us to experience an emotional state of balance.

Gratitude frames the way we experience life. Without gratitude, our fear-seeking monkey minds focus on lack. For our survival, our mind's normal state is to look for negativity so we can combat it and survive. But negativity is not a pleasurable experience, and more importantly, it does not help motivate us to the next better. Negativity tends to keep us stuck. Writing a daily gratitude list helps us to recognize the good we *do have in our life*. Again, our limbic brain focuses on fear and negativity in an attempt to keep us from harm. To counterbalance this negativity, it is necessary to actively concentrate on the good.

A daily gratitude list also frames our day *in abundance instead of lack*. If you think about it, we have so much to be grateful for—air, good health, shelter, clothing, the Internet, puppies. Our list can be our proof that things are good, full, prosperous, and abundant. It is easy to be grateful when we just received a gift, started a new relationship, or are hired for a new job. On those days when nothing is special or out of the ordinary, be grateful for all those things we take for granted like the ability to read or to have a nearby grocery store filled to the brim with tantalizing foods. When you are having a hard time finding something to be grateful for, look to your feelings of lack, and reverse them. For example, the feeling of lack, like "I wish I had a new car," could become "I am grateful for the car I have. It gets me where I need to go." Everything in our lives may not be as we want it to be, but having gratitude for what you do have opens you up to see and receive more good. When we start counting our blessings, it empowers us to expect to receive more.

Usually I start my gratitude list with something like: "Thank you for another wonderful day of life." Feel free to define the "you" as you like, such as God, spirit, universe, source, or any term resonating with you, or just use "Thanks for" to keep it anonymous. When I am feeling giddy I might write, "Thank you for letting me wake up on the green side of the grass." Then I launch into all of those things I normally take for granted, like air, food, shelter, friends, being able to walk, etc. Next, I give thanks for something wonderfully unexpected that happened the day before, like gaining a new client or getting a prime parking spot. Content can be spontaneous. Just speak from the heart.

When something truly amazing happens, I don't wait until the next morning to take note of it. I'll immediately write it down and place the paper in my gratitude jar. You don't need to have a gratitude jar, but the practice of taking a moment to notice all of the good happening through your day is powerful. As a recovering Type A, it is easy for me to pass over when something good happens, and just rush into the next thing on my to-do list. Stopping to acknowledge the good does two things for me. First, it makes me slow down. Anytime we can pause our day even for a moment, we break the momentum of stress. Second, it reframes my focus on the good in my life and affects how I go about the rest of my day. It is inspirational and energizing.

Intention

The next part of GIA is intention. Intention relates to our needs and desires outside of ourselves. Intention is about relating to others, the world, our environment, and our day-to-day life. You can create your intention statements by answering questions like:

- How do I want to relate to people?
- What do I want to accomplish today, this week, this year?
- How do I want to experience my job?
- Where do I want my business or career to go?
- What do I want to receive or own?
- Where do I want to travel?
- What do I want to attend, like a play, concert, or exhibit?

Ask yourself what you want to do, own, or have. Ask yourself how you want to be in relationship to others, such as being a powerful speaker, setting boundaries, or being charismatic. Write these statements in the present and in the affirmative, for example, "I complete the work I set out to do today."

For some it may be difficult to create intentions because they are unclear about what they want, they believe they don't deserve what they desire, or they believe their desire is impossible to have. If this occurs for you, take the negative belief that comes up for you like, "I can't afford a new iPod," and turn it into a positive intention: "I have convenient means to listen to music." Start with baby steps. If you are having a hard time paying your mortgage, setting an intention to own a mega-yacht may not be something you can imagine. Start small and obtainable. Ensure it is something you truly want and need. Next, write a statement reflecting a step in the right direction. When I started writing this book, a daily intention of "I have a completed manuscript" seemed out of reach when I hadn't yet written one word. However, writing a statement like, "I make good progress on the first chapter" was motivational and obtainable.

Many people create New Year's resolutions. "This year I am going to [fill in the blank with stop smoking, lose weight, leave my job, etc.]." The resolutions are usually built around disappointment with ourselves (I'm fat) or are a punishment (I love to smoke, but it is bad for me so I *have* to stop). Resolutions are usually based in negativity because they are about things we don't like about ourselves. Resolutions often feel like a punishment. "I love steak, but my doctor says I should stop eating red meat." Resolutions are often created to beat ourselves into submission. They are about *shoulds, have to's,* and *deprivation.* We tackle our resolutions with a vengeance, and we beat ourselves into submission. We guilt ourselves into making changes, berating our current state and setting lofty, unreachable ideals. And, usually in a few days, weeks, or months, we drop our resolutions.

Intentions are gifts to ourselves, not punishments or attacks. An intention should feel inspiring, not restrictive. When we love our selves for who and where we are, even if we want to make improvements, we create a foundation for making changes. In creating intentions, be sure they are positive, in the now, and feel good and free to you. If it feels like a punishment or an attack, either you will not move toward your desire, or you will hate every step you make toward it. A great way to reverse this is to switch from what you don't want to what you do. Instead of a resolution to stop smoking, create an intention to have healthy lungs. Instead of an intention to "lose weight," create one to "be healthy." It is much more positive, and it allows a range of ways to achieve the state of being healthy. Being healthy may mean different things at different times. Being healthy could mean eating right, saying "no" to a donut, parking farther away so you walk more, sleeping in, or a myriad of other things. Having flexibility in how you achieve your goals allows you the mental space needed to commit to achieving your goals.

Resolutions are also focused on end goals or results. Intentions are based on what we want to experience. We cannot control results, which is why resolutions fail, and we become disappointed in ourselves. When we focus on what we want to experience in the process instead of the result, we always win—because it is something we can control and achieve. Plus, we really don't want the thing or achievement; we want what such an achievement will feel like. For instance, we may think we want a red sports car, but what we really want is the feeling of exhilaration the car will provide. Disappointment and stress come in when we don't get the exact red sports car we want. However, if we focus on the experience of exhilaration, we can have the experience without the car. We could experience exhilaration in someone else's car, by skydiving, or a thousand other ways. When we focus on the experience we really want, it becomes easier to obtain it.

Important to note: intentions are focused on the "what," not the "how." A common desire is to have a certain sum of money because we believe we need to have money to buy what we want. Money is a "how." Instead of focusing on wanting a certain amount of money to buy a boat, for instance, set the intention to enjoy sailing, and watch for opportunities to be on the water. Money and owning a boat are the "how to" enjoy sailing, but we have many other ways to experience being on the water without having a boat of one's own.

Where gratitude focuses on what we have, intention and affirmation are more focused on what is to come. For some, intention, affirmation, and prayer are interchangeable. For me, I like to differentiate intention and affirmation by the type of goal, desire, or need being requested. Intention is about the physical world and our needs now. Affirmation is about our state of being.

Affirmation

Affirmation, the final part of GIA, is focused on our internal relationship with our self. Affirmations are how we want to be, how we want to act, how we want to show up, and what we want to believe. Affirmation statements can:

- **Deal with our belief of the world and how the world works.** These usually begin with "I am," such as "I am safe," or "I am guided and supported to receive good."
- **Revolve around how we see ourselves.** Examples are "I accept and embrace my full power," and "I love and approve of myself."
- **Express our desired state-of-being.** How we want to experience life, such as "I find joy in every moment."

Many people believe just writing affirmations or choosing positive words will make miraculous changes in one's life. The truth is if you do not *believe* the words, they have no power. The true power of affirmations is in deciding how you want to live and be, and choosing the thoughts, beliefs, words, and actions that reflect how you want to live. You can create your affirmation statements by looking in great books like *Heal Your Life A to Z* by Louise Hay for affirmations based on current physical illnesses. You can also create your own statements. Together, gratitude, intention, and affirmation (GIA) help to refocus our anterior cingulate cortex (ACC) on the true positives in our lives, empowering us to minimize the real and imagined stressors in our lives.

BEING TYPE ME

To be able to create intention and affirmation statements, you first need to know and accept your unique Type Me. Type Me and life purpose are very different. Life purpose is focused on a thing, a destination, or an unchanging fact. Life purpose is usually defined as a career, role, result, or achievement. Type Me is not a destination. It is not a hard, fast, physical, tangible thing we can define. Our unique Type Me is an experience.

For example, I spent over ten years in theater during school and beyond, twenty years in business, and now hopefully twenty years or more helping others. If we use the definition of life purpose as the one single career, it appears I either failed at my first careers, or I was not focused on my one true-life purpose. The truth is, my Type Me is not any of the careers I have had or currently have. The core of my Type Me is a driving force to empower others. I accomplished this by helping actors to their best performance, by mentoring my direct reports and co-workers, and now through speaking, writing, and personal sessions. My Type Me has always been with me; its outward appearance has simply looked different at various times.

What is Type Me?

• Type Me is how you are specially built to experience life, and also having the courage to live life in your unique way.

• Type Me is how the journey is taken, not where you arrive, how quickly you get there, or what riches await you at the finish line.

• Type Me is to be the best version of yourself. It is not to be a specific career, title, role, or accomplishment.

• Type Me is the best, most free, most empowered incarnation of you.

• Type Me is not about objects, roles, possessions, environments, or any other tangibles.

• Type Me is about the feelings and the experience you want.

One of the challenges is uncovering our unique Type Me within society's focus on roles and responsibilities. Society labels you as a mother, wife, CEO, room mom, parishioner, volunteer, Cubs fan, and many other titles and roles. But you are only one person. Stop wearing more than one hat. You only have one head. We struggle to try to balance all of our different roles as if each role was handled by a separate entity. This misguided thought process often causes us stress as it divides us. Instead, just wear one hat: the hat of you. Each thread in the hat is a different part of you. The threads are not just your roles, but your personality and passions. See all of these threads weaving together to make the unique you, a single hat of you. Instead of separating yourself by wearing different hats, understand yourself as a robust, multithreaded single hat.

Lately, everyone is talking about work-life balance, and how important it is to ensure work does not consume one's life. We take extra effort to ensure our personal life is given enough time and focus. But to me, the way work-life balance is usually portrayed is a misconception. It is like seeing an individual separated into mind, body, and spirit; work life and personal life are seen as separate and mutually exclusive. Do we become someone different at work, or do our preferences, beliefs, and desires exist at work as well as when we are sitting among friends and family at home? If we are out with friends, are we incapable of recognizing information we'd find helpful on the job? We are one singular being both at work and at home. We are absolutely the same person in both situations. Many people compartmentalize different aspects of themselves. They are one person at work and another at home. The issue is more than just trying to balance time between work and personal life. The core problem is we are not being our Type Me in both areas of our lives.

I see so many individuals who are unhappy with their work. They feel trapped. They feel stuck. They feel their job is sucking the life out of them. They put up with forty to sixty hours of hell for the few meager hours a week where they can live the life they love.

Cathy took it one step further. As a teacher, she wanted to be a good role model for her students. Not only did she monitor herself in the classroom, but she also let it extend into her life. What if a student sees me out acting goofy with my friends? What if a parent saw me sitting at a bar watching a ballgame? The result: Cathy kept herself from doing the things she enjoyed because she didn't think they were proper for her profession, and she thought she had to change careers in order to feel free.

Like Cathy, many of us believe we need to become something different at work, and maybe beyond. We feel a need to check our personalities, wants, and needs at the company door. We are one person at home, and when we enter the workplace, we stuff that person into the bottom drawer of our desk, along with our briefcase, until the end of the workday. The key to happiness is not ensuring we have a few hours a week to do the things we enjoy, but to begin claiming the same joy whenever and wherever we are. It means being our unique Type Me in every situation. As Cathy allowed her Type Me to be free on the weekends and appear appropriately but authentically in the classroom, she found a new joy and acceptance for her job.

Life is not one-size-fits-all. Many people seek out experts who tell them how many hours they should spend—both at work and at home. The truth is, both the number of hours, and the time of day those hours are used, depends on the individual. Morning people and night owls each have different needs and functionality. All too often we are pulled to one extreme or another. We feel obligated to live by the desires, needs, or expectations of our family, our career, our culture, and our religion. More times than not, these obligations and expectations are in conflict with each other. We feel torn between taking care of our families and taking care of work. We feel torn between the duties to our parents and the pressure of our social group. These black-and-white extremes keep us stressed and out of our Type Me.

Our unique Type Me comes in many different forms. It is our unique intersection of mind, body, and spirit. It is the point between your work and personal life, as well as the point between our needs and the needs of others. Sometimes it is difficult to uncover and embrace our personal Type Me because we are so used to wearing the roles others have given us. It can also be difficult because some beliefs we hold are not true to us. It takes a lot of courage to release our "shoulds" and "have to's" so we can accept our true Type Me. Something amazing happens when we accept our inner truth—we can fully utilize the gift that is truly us, the gift we can solely bring to the world, and the gift that will give so much to so many. Accepting and using the unique gift that is us also provides us with joy, and releases our stress for we are in alignment with our truth.

Look back through the work you completed in Awareness, Acceptance, and Alternatives.

- What clues do they give you about your Type Me?
- What things did you know and are embracing?
- What things did you know, but don't allow yourself to experience?
- What things surprised you about yourself?
- How would your experience of life be different if you truly accepted and lived in your Type Me?

Choose to accept, honor, and fully be your experiential Type Me, and see what amazing things emerge for you.

An important element in living and loving your Type Me is to shift from a results-driven mentality to being *focused on the experience.* I often work with those in job transition who find themselves stuck in the stress of choosing the right career move for them. The career they went to school for is no longer available, and they don't know what they want to do. They look at different careers, and are frustrated because none of them feel right. They are trying to fit themselves into foreign and uncomfortable roles because they are focused on income instead of passion. Job seekers often feel they need to choose from the positions they see available on the job boards. They try on job description after job description, like they are trying on a suit from a big and tall shop, when they are only five feet tall. Yes, they may be able to wear it, but it really doesn't fit them. The problem is the job seekers are starting on the outside, instead of first looking within.

The way to start within, whether you are choosing a new career, house, or mate, is to explore what it is you really want to experience. We often have a hard time choosing because we are trying to pick between things, instead of focusing on what we want to experience. True joy and the right fit is found when we focus on the experience. A great way to start knowing and embracing your Type Me is to define your experiential values.

Experiential values are the way you want to feel in life. Do you want to feel amused, peaceful, or courageous? As we have learned, we need to live life as a verb, not a noun. Life is to be experienced. Look inside yourself and determine how you prefer to experience life. Your answers are your Type Me. The only right answer is the one that is right for you. The things you enjoy, and how you enjoy life, are unique to you. If you come up with some feelings you know are right for you, but you believe them to be bad or wrong in some way, go back to Acceptance and work through your limiting beliefs. When you can identify, embrace, and focus on the experiences that truly make you happy, you will find your stress decreases the more you become in alignment with what works for you.

HABIT FORMING

As pointed out at the beginning of this book, because life changes, it is necessary to have Daily Habits to keep us centered and focused on the life we want. This is why they are Daily Habits, not one-time tools. The work in this book is not to be completed and then forgotten. It is one thing to know the road. It is something different to walk it. The practice of Awareness, Acceptance, Alternatives, and Action needs to become part of your daily routine. They are new habits to keep you living joyfully.

I encourage you not only to make a resolution to create your Type-Me Habits, but to set the intention to incorporate these habits into your daily life. I encourage you to review the previous chapters and try each Daily Habit. Pick the ones that resonate with you, and add in others you already use. Explore other options, and select the ones that make your mind, body, and soul feel better on a daily basis. As you create your personal Daily Habits, think of them as gifts to yourself, created in joy, desire, and love. Type-Me Daily Habits are something you do that make you feel better afterwards. You may need some encouragement to do them sometimes, but once you complete your Type-Me Daily Habits, you will know they were worth it.

Ensure your habits are written in joy, not personal attack. Joy empowers you to make the changes you want. Joy is a motivator. Joy creates courage and conviction. In the old adage of whether a carrot or a stick is better incentive to make a horse pull a cart, I find a carrot tends to work much better. Stop beating yourself up, and instead see the Type-Me Daily Habits you create as the life you want to experience. Your Daily Habits are a list of things you have chosen to do, and want to do. They are not a list of obligations and begrudgingly completed tasks.

Create your Daily Habits for you, not me. Make it your choice to create a new lifestyle based on new healthy habits. It doesn't matter to me if you do or don't. I know you will feel better if you do, but it is your choice. The power behind Type-Me Daily Habits is: they are uniquely yours. They are created by and for you. I have given you a starting point, but I encourage you to customize them. Just as one style of clothing does not fit each and every one of us, design your Type-Me Daily Habits to fit your life, personality, and style.

To kick off a new life of Type-Me Daily Habits, start a journal. On the first page write, "I am committing to my new habits for thirty days." It takes thirty days for new actions to become habits, and sixty days to feel like you never lived any other way. Commit to thirty days, and see how you feel. Every day record in your journal:

- What did you learn throughout the day?
- What has changed in your life?
- What has changed in your mood?
- What has changed in your relationships?
- What has changed in your career?
- What has changed in the outlook of life?

List your first Daily Habit options in your journal. Try them for a week. How faithful are you to doing them? Are there things about the habits you could tweak to make them easier to do, or provide you with a better result? Are there habits to be dropped, and new habits to be tried? Every week write them down, and at the end of the week, review how they went for you. The idea is for you to create your own Daily Habits, ones you enjoy and help you. Don't set them in stone until you know they are the ones you want. Review them every few months to see if they are still serving you, as you intended. It is not as important what the habits are, but how they affect your life, and whether they have become your new routine.

REACTING TO CONSTANT CHANGE

Part of Action is consistently moving forward, no matter the changing circumstances. Action is moment-by-moment adjustments, not a one-time event. Action is a delicate dance of constant finessing. As we are ever-changing beings in an ever-changing environment, it is very important to find and consistently engage in a daily routine, one helping us maintain our unique Type Me.

The challenge about life is that it changes. Sometimes it changes for the better, and sometimes it ushers in trials. Changes can come in the form of illness for you, a job loss or position shift, losing someone close, divorce, or some other critical, urgent, and all-consuming difficulty. Changes can also come in the form of a new position, a new love, a new home, or a new adventure. Whatever the change, it shakes your routine. It can knock out your balance. It can change the priorities in your life. If you lose your job, your focus is pulled to finding a new career and managing your finances, which can mean you are no longer focusing on your intimate relationships. Or the illness of a loved one pulls you away from your own self-care. Whatever the change, be extra vigilant about maintaining your Daily Habits.

It is easy to assume your Daily Habits are not important when you have an emergency at work, or with your family. We often tell ourselves the crisis or someone else's needs deserve our attention and take priority over our own. This is actually the time to strengthen your Daily Habits. These habits are the grounding tools of your life and will help you make it through life's challenges. Maintaining your Daily Habits helps you manage the ups, downs, and changes of everyday life.

Imagine not being able to drink water from sunup to sundown. Think you could do it? It may be easy to go without water during a cold, snowy winter, but imagine not being able to quench your thirst during a hot summer day. The same holds true for your Type-Me practice. When things are going well, it may be easy to maintain your practices. But when your job has an important deadline, a friend needs to go to the doctor, or your car breaks down, finding time for the State of Gray, and having the ability to practice gratitude, may be difficult. It is okay. Do the best you can. Be sure to be diligent when things are good so you can begin to make your Type-Me Habits true habits.

When things are more challenging, gently and compassionately encourage yourself to maintain your practice as much as you can. Your daily habits will be the foundation for limiting your stress. Instead of putting your habits aside and focusing on the emergency, first reach for your habits. Use them as a tool to keep you centered and clear. In doing so, you will find the stress you are experiencing is minimized and easier to handle. The Type-Me Habits are your crutch when times are tough. Use them. For more support during your journey to becoming Type Me, sign up to receive supportive and inspirational newsletters (www.DownloadTypeMe.com).

THE SPIRAL OF LIFE

The other day I caught up with a client I had a few years earlier. I was thrilled to hear he had continued his practice. When I first met James, he was a high-strung executive who was having a difficult time 1) balancing multiple business responsibilities, 2) wanting to strengthen his relationship with his family, 3) needing more time for self-care, and 4) feeling he had to have a certain appearance (car, house, title) to maintain his friendships. James was now truly loving and creating his life. He was still practicing his Type-Me Daily Habits. He uncovered, accepted, and truly embraced his Type Me, doing so no matter what his friends were doing, or what he thought he needed to do. Focusing on his true needs, James was able to move easily between work and home, enjoying both. He was choosing what was best for him, not what he "should" do. It wasn't always an easy path, as he admitted some frustration about the transition to his new life and the time it took, but he said it was like winning the lottery. When people win a ton of money, it is often overwhelming. They don't know how to deal with it, and often lose it all. Life is a journey. Each change helps you learn, grow, and have the power for the next change. If, like winning the lottery, we were hit with major changes all at once, it would be too much. Instead, it is important to embrace a series of baby steps.

Be patient with yourself on your journey. At times, you may find you are revisiting the same issue, lesson, or opportunity you experienced before. However, each time we come to the same crossroads, it is different. Life is not linear. I see it as an ascending spiral. Issues or challenges we face run vertically alongside the spiral. We move along the path of the spiral, and we will see reoccurring challenges and issues, but they really are different each time because we are different. We are at a different age, in a different relationship, and have different knowledge, experiences, and perspectives. The environment these lessons are occurring in is different, the players may be different, or there could be a myriad of different situational changes. Each time the issues occur, they give us a chance to learn and grow deeper. We have not failed if we are faced by a similar challenge. We are simply deepening the lesson of the challenge.

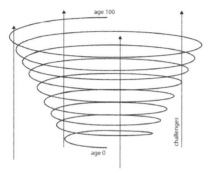

It is important to look at each challenge as new, even if it feels like you have been there before. Don't be hard on yourself if you are back to square one with an issue. Are you really?

- Do you notice a new facet of the experience?
- Is it a lesson you haven't learned, or one you can now strengthen by repeating the experience?
- Are there tools you have now you didn't have then you can now use to solve the problem once and for all?
- What deeper learning can you receive this time through?
- How does having this issue rear its head again propel you closer toward your ultimate Type Me?
- What snow (stress, issue) did you not shovel/uncover last time this issue appeared?
- How do you benefit from addressing this issue again?

When I was in graduate school for directing, one instructor spoke about his first professional play. When his mentor came backstage and asked him what he thought, he said it went well, but he made a few mistakes in his directing choices. He was confident he would not make the same mistakes in the future. His mentor wisely smiled and said, "No, you will still make them. You will just catch them sooner." The same goes for us. We may still fall into old ways of being, but know that each time you do, you will catch yourself earlier and earlier. Soon you will be able to catch yourself in the moment, allowing you to make new choices immediately.

At different times of your life, you may be faced with difficult challenges, but hopefully through the Type-Me concepts, you handle the challenges better. Many who sell the "silver-bullet" concept promise a life of continuous great ease and brilliance. This is unrealistic. Everything in nature has highs and lows, easy times and difficult ones. Just like low and high tide or the four seasons, your life will have highs, lows, times of growth, and times of dormancy. Peace comes from accepting, not fighting these changes. Fighting causes pain. Accepting and moving through these seasons and obstacles provides peace. Does a tree fight when its leaves turn brown and fall? Or does it gracefully release its leaves in the fall, accepting the loss because this act will provide the rest and revitalization it will need to bud and grow the next season? Even nature at times seems to be violent and destructive, but it continues the cycle of growth. Wildfires in the southwest can be horrendous. Yet without the fires, there would be no new growth of trees. Pinecones need the heat in order to seed, so the seeming destruction of the fires is actually birthing new trees. The fires also remove the larger, older trees so the younger, smaller trees can have their chance to grow. Seeming disaster and destruction is an important component of growth.

The same is true for us. Sometimes we need to go through a seasonal shift, or an all-out fire, to progress to new growth. Nothing in life remains the same. Let go of your expectation life will be consistent. Just like we let go of our constant seeking for some future outcome, it is important to let go of creating a false sense of security and stability. Only in the movie *Groundhog Day* did the same day repeat and repeat and repeat. And if you saw the movie, you also know the lead character was driven crazy by experiencing sameness again and again. Life is meant for challenges, growth, learning, giving, and change. Embrace it. Run head first into challenges instead of running from them. Might as well. The truth is, the challenge will find you even when you try to hide.

You have all the tools you need to reduce your stress. Now, ask yourself if you are ready to make your personal Type-Me Habits a daily part of your life so you reduce your stress levels and create the life you want. You have the power to create the experience of life you desire. Spend some time defining what you want to experience, and use your daily tools to begin making that experience a reality for you. You have the ability to create the life you want. All you need to do is choose to act.

CLIENT'S TYPE-ME STORY: IT IS . . . AND ALWAYS WAS MY CHOICE

By Sam Hull

At first glance, my early forties brought me nothing but despair. My business had dried up, my artistic endeavors were nonexistent, and I was in a never-ending cycle of helping other people with *their* projects. I felt my body had turned against me with bad feet, multiple kidney stones, and an unexplained vertigo that locked me in a chair for four months straight. To top it off, my two dog children passed within four months of each other. My life was full of drama, pain, and loss.

My partner had accepted an ideal job in his field, so I had given up a tenure-track professorship to move across the country. My family and friends who consider Oregon the other side of the world were upfront about their reluctance to visit the Northwest, and questioned why I would choose to leave Florida. I didn't see it as a choice, but as a necessity, something expected of me, something spouses did to support the family. Everyone was telling me I had made my life about my husband and had given up my own goals. Looking back I can admit I was excited to leave Florida for many reasons, but I had not considered my identity or career in accepting the move.

Initially, I was able to create a thriving design business in Oregon, but as the economy fell apart, I no longer found the dream projects with unlimited budgets to which I had become accustomed. In fact, my business went from dream budgets to its end pretty quickly. Initially, I had contacted Melissa for guidance when I was feeling down, and consciously I was seeing the end of my business nearing. In retrospect, I am sure I was also subconsciously aware that my older dog, Kiki, was starting her departure, too. My friends had joked for years about who would check me into the asylum when that dreaded day came. I felt like the world was coming after me. I knew I should have options, but they were hard to see.

Working with Melissa, she explained to me *what a choice really was.* I kept thinking, and probably saying too, "I am educated. I have been a university professor for many years. I have three college degrees, for the love of God. I know what making a choice is, Melissa." Angrily, I read some books she suggested, and we talked on the phone. I wrote some lists, and did some exercises for my brain, all the while thinking, "This is bullshit since the world is the problem. I should just give her the names of the people causing me problems, pay to have her call them, and get the counseling to the right people." I really thought that might be a solution. I was so far down the rabbit hole at the time I could not acknowledge my own thoughts and actions, only the events and chaos happening to me. But as Kiki grew more ill and I began to worry and fear, my theory of victimhood started to fall apart. I knew Kiki would never intentionally cause me pain. She would not cause me such anguish. I could no longer deny that I was melting down all on my own. It was unmistakable; I was somehow the cause of my emotional collapse, and probably a huge factor in my physical one, too.

During another session, I heard Melissa say again, *"Why are you choosing this,* Sam?" and this time for whatever reason, it was clear. I had no answer, but I finally heard her.

Kiki passed; the next week was silent around the house. I had extreme anxiety attacks, I couldn't sleep, and surprisingly I became afraid to be alone. I made lists, angry lists of what I felt wronged about, and detailed lists of people with whom I was disappointed. I wrote down names of clients I hated working with, personal projects I never finished, and my dreams I never started. I had pages full of sacrifices I felt I had made to keep my nineteen-year marriage going. I am telling you, I had a notebook full of remorse, bitterness, and fury. I cried, I screamed, I pleaded, and then one random Tuesday, I heard Melissa's voice in my head, and I asked myself, *"Why did you choose this?"* The answers I came up with varied between things "expected" of me, things I felt "had" to be done, and the things only "I" could do. In hindsight, my Midwest upbringing came with many rules and things good people "should" do, and everything I felt obligated to do had gotten the best of me. Clear and simple, I had just done what I had been trained to do, and it had all happened while I was on autopilot.

The next several months were full of *choices.* I cut all kinds of people from my life. I said "No," "Hell NO," and even threw in an occasional "Why are you calling me about this

crap?" It felt great. The more I scratched off my lists, the better I felt. I took the word "should" out of my vocabulary, and
examined what I had been programmed to believe versus what
I chose to believe.

Then my other dog, Zeus, got sick. He had stopped eating
two months after Kiki passed, but being a hearty Shih Tzu of
numerous extra pounds, the vet felt it would pass. "Grief," the
vet said, "is hard on dogs who never leave their mothers." A
few weeks later, I could not avoid the obvious: things were not
getting better for Zeus, and he was slipping away. I panicked,
but from working with Melissa, I was able to grasp that Zeus
had made a decision. He was *choosing* not to eat. I could put
bacon in his mouth, and he would gently lay it on the floor and
lick his lips. Zeus always loved bacon, but he didn't want it.
He was working on a plan.

In the end, Zeus went eight weeks with no food. He
dropped from twenty-six pounds to nine pounds, and I had
to choose to let him go. It was clear he would allow himself to
waste away. On Valentine's Day, in pain, he gave me *the look,*
and I called the vet. My husband arrived home from work with
surprise flowers, candy, and a smile to find me holding Zeus
and informing him the vet would be here in fifteen minutes to
put Zeus down. The old me would have waited another day.
You just shouldn't do this sort of thing willingly on Valentine's
Day. It's just not done. But the new me, the person who was
making choices in his life, was more attuned to what Zeus had
chosen, and gave him the only thing I could on this day of love:
compassion. The next few weeks were rough, but I didn't roll
over and die.

I slipped a few times and blamed the world for my quiet
house, my sleepless nights, and my short temper. I grew tired
of the need to find something to do. It was grief, and it was

normal. I swore no new pets for a year. Yet, four months later we rescued from a kill shelter a wonderful dog we call Pippin. He is amazing and has started to heal my heart. I had to make a conscious choice to love Pippin, as my instinct told me it was cheating on the memory of Kiki and Zeus. I had made up this story to explain my grief, but grief just is; it doesn't have to make sense. Next, I gathered the strength to face my health issues, which I put off due to fear. For eight years, I had struggled with foot issues due to an unwillingness to acknowledge my limitations and choose a treatment plan. As I heal from the surgery now, I know it was the right choice, one I made to improve my life.

My work with Melissa has been a simple question, but one with profound actions. "Why do you choose (*fill in the blank*)?" One answer will lead to another, I can assure you. Some answers are painful, some are fun, and others trivial. But a life full of choices is better than a life of unconscious actions and self-victimization. At my worst, I simply let things happen; I passively completed tasks and held on to my identity through my pets and social status. Losing my dog children was my bottom, but it was also my resurrection because I had Melissa in my life urging me to "*choose.*" I chose to take the next step, I chose to take the next breath, and I chose to take responsibility for my own happiness.

LESSONS LEARNED

• Real and imagined fears cause stress and can be addictive.

• To combat anxiety and fear, use the power of GIA (gratitude, intention, and affirmations) to retrain the survival brain.

• Type Me is your unique way of being, and should be present no matter the circumstances.

• Daily Habits are self-created motivators, not another to-do.

• Daily Habits keep you grounded and clear, no matter what life throws at you.

DAILY HABIT OPTIONS

• A daily *Gratitude List* (see pp. 170) can help strengthen your ACC and create a more positive outlook.

• Use a *Gratitude Jar* (see pp. 170) to stop and actively recognize when good enters your life.

• *Random Appreciation* (see pp. 171) is a deep dive into gratitude.

• Take some time to uncover and embrace your *Intentions* (see pp. 171).

• Keep stress from building up by taking a *Pause* (see pp. 173) during the day.

GRATITUDE LIST

Every morning write down everything you are grateful for from the day before. Take stock of your life right now. Write down everything you have for which you are grateful. Try to spend at least five minutes creating your inventory.

Don't have time or are you especially stressed? Before you get out of bed, think of three things for which you are grateful. This is a great way to pause, focus on the good, and start your day off positively.

GRATITUDE JAR

To record those special, amazing gifts that happen throughout the day, create a system to record them immediately. A client gifted me with a mason jar, and to it are clipped slips of paper. When something amazing happens, I grab a slip of paper and write down the reason I am grateful. Take a moment to recognize the gratitude before adding the slip to the mason jar. It's nice when I am having a bad day, or feel like everything is going wrong, to empty the jar and read all of the amazing things happening for me.

RANDOM APPRECIATION
Write down two or three random things, places, and/or people.

1.
2.
3.

For each item, spend five minutes journaling about what you appreciate about it. Practiced daily, this random appreciation will brighten your day, and keep you focused on the power of appreciation. It will also help you see something to be grateful for when you are in a challenging situation.

INTENTIONS
Over two to three weeks, go into the State of Gray and fill out what is important to you in each of the categories below. Take your time, and allow intuition and guidance to help you fill out the sheet as it comes to you over time.

• Career
• Community
• Financial
• Friends and Family
• Fun and Recreation

- Health
- Intimate Relationships
- Mental / Emotional Health
- Personal Growth
- Physical Environment
- Spirituality

In each of these areas above, note the things:
- You feel are currently making you happy.
- You need to leave behind.
- You want to bring in. Try not to think of the *how* you will get them, just that they are desired.

When you have clarity, use the prompts below to write down what you want for the next twelve months. Fill out as much as you can.

How I want to be:
- Why do I want it?
- Actions that will help me get there?

What I want to do:
- Why do I want it?
- Actions that will help me get there?

What I want to have:
- Why do I want it?
- Actions that will help me get there?

Every day, write your intentions for the day. Intentions are written in joy and positivity. They are focused on the experience, and not the thing. Intentions are also written in the present tense. Do not use "hope" or "will have." Intentions are written as if they have already been obtained. Intentions are also obtainable. If you have a large dream or desire, break it down to just what you can imagine, or what you desire for today. This will help you see it as a reality.

Here is a standard format for an intention.

I (present tense verb like "am"—do not use "will," "hope," "may," or any other conditional verb) *then your desired experience.*

Throughout the day, you can ask yourself if what you are doing is helping you to experience your intention. If not, what can you shift to be more in alignment with your desire?

PAUSE

A powerful tool to help you maintain your Type-Me Habits, and to keep stress from building up, is to add pauses to your day. One of the ways stress gains the upper hand is because we continue to chase it. We rush from one project to the next. We jump from one worry to another. Building pauses into your day short-circuits stress buildup, and resets your mental clarity.

Here are a few ways to build pauses into your day.

• **Stop before each meal and give thanks**. This allows you to be mindful about what you are eating, uses gratitude to reframe your mind, and gives you a pause a few times a day.

• **Set your watch**. Set an alarm to go off a few times a day as a reminder to pause.

• **Let it be spontaneous**. Choose something that frequently happens like receiving text messages. Every time you receive a text, take a breath before responding. This can also slow down the frantic nature of instant technology.

• **Move it**. Take a walk. Park far away from your office, or take the stairs to add some time and space away from work and responsibilities.

• **Put it down.** When you are talking to a live human being, put down the phone, tablet, and computer, and focus solely on your conversation.

CHAPTER 7

Take Back Your Life

*There came a time when the risk to remain tight in the bud was
more painful than the risk it took to blossom.*
— Anais Nin, French-Cuban author

The largest obstacle to the message of releasing stressful Type-A behaviors is that people, myself included, don't seem to be willing to act until they hit rock bottom with an illness, layoff, divorce, or other debilitating event. Unfortunately, since we 1) live much of our lives on autopilot, 2) have created schedules that do not allow any breathing room, 3) believe stress and strain are normal parts of life, 4) are bound to roles and responsibilities, and 5) define our self-worth and a sense of pride in being busy, we never take the time to analyze if our lives are truly pleasing to us, nor do we explore if we have other options. Please do not wait until the stress you feel negatively affects some or all areas of your life. These simple Type-Me Habits can make a difference in your experience even *before* things are too difficult to handle.

I hope you have gleaned from these lessons the benefits you can receive right now. You no longer need to experience stress, struggle, worry, or anxiety every day. Type Me can be a more enjoyable way to approach life. It is within your power to become *Aware* of your thoughts, beliefs, actions, and reactions; *Accept* the circumstances, issues, and people in your life; uncover *Alternatives* that better serve how you would like to live, and take *Action* toward a more fulfilling, less stressful life. I hope you learned how this process can release the real you from extreme Type A-ism, and empower you to make the choices to best serve you. Through adopting and personalizing the Type-Me Habits, you can change your daily existence for the better, living with less stress, powerfully, authentically, and joyfully.

TIMING IS EVERYTHING

The Type-Me Habits can be intimidating and overwhelming to some. If you are in the midst of a crisis, are a hardcore Type A, or feel strong resistance to this program, it's okay. Choose one tool, not even a full Daily Habit. Don't try to do them all. Just find one tool or mind shift to help you right now. My journey to Type Me was not just the result of my experience in Peru. Decades of work, realizations, awakenings, and healings led me to being ready to do the work in Peru, and for years afterward.

Be gentle with yourself. Look at where you are in your journey. Remember this is a journey, not a destination. See where you are right now and how you can make it just a little bit better. Do not make the Type-Me Habits another checkbox on your to-do list. You have learned the tools needed to make your life better. Bring these tools into your life when and how you need them. The goal is for you to be Type Me, *your Type Me*. It may take time for this to happen.

If any of the habits now or in the future feel like a stressful to-do, don't do it. They are tools to reduce your stress, not add more. Remember, this is a new way to be. I have provided options and possibilities for you, but it is up to you to decide how they fit into your Type-Me life. If a habit helps you enjoy the experience of life, do it daily. If a habit adds stress and strain, it is not right for you.

Ben is a favorite client of mine. He is a real go-getter. When we met, he had already made some life changes to bring him into better alignment with his Type Me. He would grasp and implement the lessons from each session. Ben was becoming more Aware, more Accepting. He chose appropriate Alternatives for his Type Me and took daily Actions to integrate these learnings into his life. As he progressed, he gave me a sweet thank-you card: "You are an inspiration to me, and have helped me more than I can ever articulate." But Ben's life was busy. Overly busy. Due to previous commitments and a new business venture, his days were packed. Thankfully he also scheduled and made time for the things needed to feed his soul, but the result was every hour of the day was scheduled.

Ben knew he wanted to go deeper into his Type-Me work. He knew he still needed to take more control over his commitments and schedule, but he couldn't because he simply did not have enough hours in the day. And that is okay. Ben can use the habits he has already developed to help him balance his needs versus responsibilities, and he calls on the tools he needs when a major stressor appears, but this is not the time for any future work. Once his responsibilities lessen, he will be able to enter into deeper work.

The same goes for you. Timing is everything. Start utilizing those tools and habits available to help you right now, wherever you are. As you begin to implement even the smallest part of the Type-Me lessons, you will begin to make a shift in your life. The shift may be fast, or it could take years to complete. Either is acceptable. Go at your pace, and do what resonates with you. Remember you have no end goal. Your success in this program is to improve your experience every day, and in doing so, *you win.*

RECOVERING TYPE A

I call myself a Recovering Type A, because I am. To write this book I had pages of checklists helping me stay on track. I balanced writing a book with my client schedule, radio show, and family responsibilities. These days I am just as busy, if not more, than I ever was. I still rely on my checklists and schedules. The difference is now I am in control of what I am doing, instead of having what I am doing control me. I have not lost my Type-A tendencies—I am simply more aware of them, and if they are not serving me, I adjust them.

The other day I was hounding my husband to fill out some paperwork. It had been on my list for weeks, and I wanted it done. In the past, I would have become a tyrant, forcing him to do the work, being upset when he didn't, and chastising him for taking so long. This time I caught myself. I stopped to consider why this was so important to me. After reflection, I realized it was not so important to me. Checking the box to show it was completed was important. Upon realizing this, I could relax and let go of my self-created deadline. And my husband was grateful.

The goal of the Type-Me Habits is not to eradicate all of your Type-A behaviors. The goal is to put you into the driver's seat of the behaviors. Be aware of your tendencies. Don't feel a victim of them. Notice when they happen, and whether they serve you. And if they don't, take action to minimize their negative effect. Do not chastise yourself when they pop up. You will have negative Type-A behaviors pop up on occasion. It is important you notice the behaviors and choose to correct them, providing you with stress relief and a feeling of freedom.

MAKE IT REAL

In Jim Collins's book *Good to Great*, Admiral Stockdale recounts his survival in a POW camp. His ability to survive when those around him did not was because he was realistic about his situation, and was conscious and present in his daily activities. He was engaged in Acceptance and the State of Gray. Those around him who were optimistic about a rescue found themselves disappointed and depressed when it did not happen. Others who were pessimistic about their situation lost their spirit and will to live, and they were easily broken. Admiral Stockdale's realistic consistency kept him going. And so it will be with your practice.

To make the Type-Me Habits work for you, make them a "want to," not a "need to." Have a genuine desire to adopt new habits, and actively create the life you want to experience. Find the habits that resonate with you, and are a joy and a support, not a punishment or restriction. Embrace them and make them yours. Gift yourself with these tools to make your life better and less stressful.

Type-Me Habits do not fix you—because you are not broken. Remember, *you are* a worthy, complete, and perfect person. Nothing is wrong, crazy, or damaged within you. These habits are just tools to allow you to adjust how you think, believe, speak, act, and react. In making adjustments to your behaviors, you can affect what you experience for the better. Do not enter into blame, attack, or victimization. You are wonderful right now, and on the verge of becoming even better.

You are powerful. Each of us is responsible for and empowered to affect our lives for the better. Joy is found in the act of living, and being in the present moment. You have the power to choose your experience. Have the courage to look for and correct the root problem, not the symptom. This will provide you with lasting positive changes. Your life can be improved by changing your thoughts, beliefs, perceptions, actions, and reactions, not by changing circumstances or other people. The Type-Me Habits of Awareness, Acceptance, Alternatives, and Actions are your unique, customizable framework for power. The way to take back and maintain a joy-filled life is by working at it each and every moment of every day.

You now hold all the tools you need to make long-lasting changes to your life for the better. But knowing is not enough. It is now time to act. I encourage you to decide to embrace the Type-Me Habits, selecting ones meaningful and helpful to you. Start using them every day. Release the notion that your life needs to be busy, stressful, and hectic. Know you can still accomplish many things, while being centered. You can still be productive, and take care of yourself. You can still handle all of your roles and responsibilities, but you can do this from a state of joy and calm. Are you ready to try a different way to be?

Join others on their journey to becoming Type Me by giving and receiving support in the Facebook group at www. LiveTypeMe.com

My Journey
from Type A to Type Me

At first I didn't know why I felt so poorly. I thought it might be because my new job was filled with travel, deadlines, and major projects. My stress levels increased while my exercise decreased. My eating habits became poor when processed, prepackaged convenience foods and the perceived need for caffeine became the norm. Even when I tried to eat better, the weight still kept coming on, and my digestive system was erratic. I began to have health issues with seemingly no known source. My menstrual cycle was horrendous with heavy flowing for weeks, not days, excruciating pain piercing into my legs, a bloated, protruding stomach, an agonizingly constricted back, plus a slew of digestive problems. I was tired, drained, and irritable. First, I searched for relief from this pain with all the doctors in my HMO: gynecologists, urologists, and gastroenterologists. They poked, prodded, and prescribed. Each had an idea of how to relieve my symptoms, but again and again they could not diagnose the source of my pain. No doctor could find the *cause* of my illness. They did their best to pump me full of prescription drugs in the hope it would solve my severe discomfort, bloating, and irregularity, all to no avail. Finally, one doctor suggested a hysterectomy *might* relieve my pain. I didn't think "might" constituted enough reason for surgery, and so I left all the allopathic specialists behind.

After getting nowhere with Western medicine doctors, I was now open to exploring the world of homeopathic medicine. My first stop was acupuncture. By holding my wrist and looking at my tongue, the acupuncturist diagnosed my qi, the circulating life force of Chinese medicine, was too warm. He said my yin was overpowering my yang, or was it the other way around? In any case, I received a slew of specifically made herbs and was stuck with needles a few times a week. Initially, I felt some relief, which soon appeared to plateau. I also wanted to know why my qi was so hot. Why was I out of balance? What was the root cause?

Onward I went, this time to a nutritionist. When my hormone levels were tested, it reflected the same imbalance found by the acupuncturist. Another round of herbs, vitamins, and supplements were administered. I followed the program without fail, popping tablets before every meal, making changes to what I ate, as well as how and when I ate, adding in exercise, and even hiring a personal trainer. Again I found some initial comfort, but no true relief.

During this physical crisis, I was also still receiving regular chiropractic adjustments and massages to manage the back pain from a car accident. The massage therapist I frequented often told me of the trips she took to Peru to work with a shaman. Face down on the table I would listen to her stories of plant medicine and energetic healings. It was pretty far-out information. She was very into it, and her passion made the stories very interesting to hear, but energy work, shamans, and ancient culture weren't my thing. However, one day in 2007, she shared a story of this shaman curing a man with cancer. It caught my attention. Since I was running out of options for my own health, I began to consider this might be a valid course of action, or at least as valid as taking out organs and digesting chemicals. In a moment of desperation, I thought traveling over three thousand miles, and working with a South American shaman, might be my last hope.

The seed was planted. I was considering flying to Peru to be healed, but it was a hard decision. Could this mystic healer help me where all the others had failed? Could I go alone to a country where I had never been before? Could I justify taking such an expensive trip? I used every decision tool I could think of to justify the trip, but it just did not seem to make sense. Yet the idea of going would not leave me. I remember the day I decided to go. It was not based on logical justification. My heart, soul, intuition, and desperation just called out, "Go!" Thankfully my husband, being ever supportive, had no issue with me going, and he also hoped I would find the relief I was seeking.

A 3,000-MILE JOURNEY INWARD

In the month before leaving for Peru, I was instructed to consume a very strict diet. No caffeine, chocolate, alcohol, red meat, spicy foods, citrus, plus many, many more no-no's. I think I had chicken, rice, and green vegetables for dinner every night. It wasn't easy, but I did feel better following this menu. The restricted diet was mandatory in order to be able to work with plant medicines. Like peyote of the American Indians, Peruvian shamans use San Pedro and Ayahuasca cactus for energetic, spiritual journeys and healings. It was important to have our systems ready to accept the power of the plants. If not, I'd be vomiting a lot. I preferred to follow the diet.

The ever-ardent student, I purchased a journal specifically for the trip so I could make the most of the work we would do. I wanted to record how to release all of the physical, emotional, and psychological pain I was experiencing. In the front page of the journal I wrote my intentions for the trip: Love Myself, Forgive Myself, Take Care of Myself, Be Fearless, and Be Worry-Free.

With one oversized backpack, a water-filtration bottle, and a floppy hat, I headed to Peru. Flying to a foreign country alone to meet up with a group of people I didn't know was a little nerve-racking. At the airport, the check-in clerk told me about his 1990 trip to Peru where the rebel group Sendero Luminoso put a machine gun to his chest asking for his documents. Well, something to look forward to, I thought. In the Miami airport where I met my flight to Lima, I connected with some of the other group members, including a married couple from Tennessee and two women from the Midwest. All were in the Baby Boomer age range, and appeared very granola, hippy, and earthy. My Corporate America–speak seemed very out of place.

After over seven hours in the air, we landed in Peru. As Lima is in the same time zone as Chicago, I appreciated not having to go through jetlag after the long flight. Upon landing I fell into my caretaker role as I helped the rest of the group find their luggage, change money, and maneuver two airports. You would have thought I was the tour guide instead of a fellow tourist.

Waiting for the connecting flight to Cusco, the altitude (eleven thousand feet above sea level) started to kick in, and I became a little dizzy. The flight to Cusco was interesting. The airplane took off, and just continued to ascend. I don't think we came down to land in Cusco; we just stopped climbing. Outside the plane window, I could see the barren mountains of Peru's August winter. The desert winter dust hung on the mountains, and scant buildings dotted the landscape here and there. I preferred the Peruvian winters of dust, mild days, and colder nights once the sun set, versus the freezing, snowy cold of an Illinois winter.

After landing and grabbing our luggage, we took a bus from the airport to Poqen Kanchay, my home for the next two weeks. Looking out the window, I was stunned by the abject poverty of this developing country. Not even a mile from the airport, a woman walked up a steep hillside loaded with heavy kindling on her back as two sheep faithfully followed behind her. About thirty people gathered by a dirty stream near the railroad tracks. Women appeared to be washing laundry in the river made dark by the Peruvian winter dust. Families surrounded large hanging blankets. I could not tell if the blankets strung up on lines were just drying, or if they were shelter for the evening. My heart broke for these people. The poorest homeless person in the United States seemed rich in comparison.

Winter dust also covered the buildings of Cusco and San Jeronimo. They appeared dirty, worn-out, and in need of some major TLC. We came to a corner and someone said, "There it is. Poqen Kanchay." There? There it is? The building was made of simple unpainted handmade concrete and was covered with the thick dust of Peruvian winters. What had I gotten myself into? Would my accommodations be just a modest step above those of the people we had seen near the river? As we walked from the bus into the courtyard, I felt like I was Dorothy in *The Wizard of Oz*. Nothing inside was like the dingy black and white of the outside. The courtyard instead surrounded us with a lush garden filled with irises, roses, and other beautiful flowers and plants. The walls of the courtyard were gaily painted in bright earthen colors of orange, yellow, and green. A smiling staff greeted us, immediately rushing to take our bags, and hand us a cup of warm tea. Accustomed to taking care of myself, I tried to carry my own bag, but I was not allowed. At first I thought it was Latino male courtesy, but the longer I was there, the more I eased into the new experience of being cared for completely and unconditionally.

We were treated to a sumptuous lunch. The first course was avocado with spinach sauce. Next was an egg drop–type soup with vegetables, including enormous corn kernels as large as my thumbnail. Finally, the meal finished with fried chicken, pota-

toes, and a garlic-tomato-cucumber dish. Afterwards, we gathered in the common area to witness a dispacho ceremony led by
two local shamans. The shamans looked as if they were ripped
from a page out of *National Geographic*. Their faces were wrin-
kled from years living with the land, and their dark, thin bodies
were cloaked in intricately hand-woven ponchos. The ceremony
to ensure success for our journey was all in the Quechua language
and consisted of some songs, chants, and a burnt offering. Some
of the other group members had brought down altar cloths and
prayer stones for the ceremony. It seemed odd to me that hearty
Americans would have the accoutrements of a South American
religion. The artwork in the group room and dining hall was
an interesting mix between Incan artifacts and Christian sym-
bolism. During the ceremony, I couldn't help but wonder if the
three coca leaves of the kintu were really the Inca spiritual worlds,
or if they represented the Christian trinity, or maybe both. Almost every day during my trip, fireworks were held in celebration
of some Christian event like a saint's day or the Pope's birthday.
Everywhere I looked I saw a blending of these two belief systems.

After a light dinner of soup and dessert, I slept well until six
o'clock the next morning. Most mornings I was the first to rise,
so the entire courtyard garden was mine to enjoy. The ever-present mate de coca (coca leaf tea) was usually ready to brew, and I
would enjoy a cup while journaling before breakfast. I cherished
my quiet time in the mornings. I could soak in the natural beauty
of the garden while reflecting on the previous day's events. With
a sip of tea to awaken my body, I would journal, processing all I
had learned, before setting my intentions for the day ahead.

The plan for our second day was a cleansing to take place in
the city of San Pedro. Naively I expected this to be a ritualistic
ceremony like the one the night before. Nope. This time we were
to participate in a communal event using agua minero medicinal

(medicinal mineral water). It was not explained at the time, but from what I now understand Peru has many medicinal springs, each having a different healing purpose. A person floats in some springs to relieve muscle spasms, and some springs are consumed to treat different maladies, from blood diseases to respiratory issues. Since the water we drank was yellow and bubbly, my guess is we experienced mineral waters infused with sodium, calcium, iron, and different forms of bicarbonates. We arrived at the San Pedro municipal park and paid about one U.S. dollar each for a glass and toilet paper. We all filled our cups with bubbling mineral water, drinking glass after glass until we needed to defecate. It was a cleansing all right.

I don't know if it was because I was such a tight-ass control freak unwilling to let go, or because of my fear of public outhouses, but I had almost twenty glasses before making my first trip to the "bathroom." The toilet facilities were two rows of unisex stalls. Inside each stall were two metal footprints. One was to stand on the footprints, drop trou, and let 'er rip. Afterwards, the user grabbed a bucket of city water to wash away any leftovers. Never having done this before, I was really concerned about how good my aim was, as I didn't want to come back with discolored pants, shoes, or socks. For four hours at the location, and for another four hours later, the power of this natural colonic did its trick. I was very happy I had followed the month-long diet before participating in this experience. The diet helped clean my system partially beforehand, so it was not so intense for me. Others in our group were not as lucky.

The experience at San Pedro was the first time I met Don Theo, the owner and shaman of Poqen Kanchay. He was very different from the shamans we met the first day. Don Theo appeared very European and distinguished. He had dark Peruvian features, but usually dressed in khaki pants, a corduroy sports jacket, a scarf, and a felt hat. He looked more like a reporter for *National Geographic* than a native pictured in the magazine. Don Theo, educated in archeology and politics, was still involved in both. He was a modern renaissance man who moved easily between the modern physical world and the ancient spiritual world. Don Theo only joined us at spiritual sites, the cleansing, and during plant ceremonies; then he would disappear. He was a quiet but knowledgeable man with a kindness in his eyes, yet he also felt distant and detached in some ways. Our group was organized by two American tour guides and was managed by the ever-present Pepe. Pepe was a sweet man who told me the first day at Poqen Kanchay that my Spanish, which I used simply to say "*hola*," was very good, and he would only speak to me in Spanish. Little did he know "*hola*" was about the only thing I could remember from my high school Spanish class.

After the mineral water cleansing, we all went to the ancient site of Raqchi. While there, we huddled in the remnants of a round hut. Someone began humming, and the others joined in. It was a vibrationally resonant hum, not a bubbly top-forty hit. I didn't know what was going on. I guess I should have known we'd have spiritual practices during this trip, but my focus was solely on finding physical relief, so it didn't cross my mind. Anyway, the group was humming, and when I also tried, I could feel the vibration in my chest. At one point it felt like the sound was not coming from me but from an existence all its own, but maybe it was just the altitude messing with me. As we finished touring this site, we saw five fountains springing up from a stone slab. They were so interesting because no one has been able to track the original source of the water, even after following the trail for over one hundred kilometers into the mountains.

HEALING

Day three brought with it my first experience with San Pedro—the cactus, not the city. San Pedro is a medicinal cactus used for thousands of years in the Andes. The cactus contains mescaline, a known psychedelic drug. During the Spanish conquest, the Roman Catholic Church tried to stop its use but instead, like most of the current culture in Peru, ancient traditions and Christianity blended. The cactus was dubbed San Pedro because Saint Peter (San Pedro) holds the keys to heaven, and the cactus is used to "unlock the gates of heaven on earth."

After a large breakfast, Don Theo talked about how making judgments, even pleasant ones, can lead to pain. When we make judgments we are classifying not only the item we are talking about, but also all other items in the same category. For instance, if we say we like blue, it implies we dislike other colors. If I say you are beautiful, it infers everyone else is ugly. We judge others by what we experienced when we were younger. We make the assumption everyone has had the exact same childhood as we did, and therefore they should act, think, and believe the same as us. Doesn't everyone have two parents of different genders who never divorced? Didn't everyone grow up in a single-family house with a large yard? Aren't people with different religions, parental situations, or homes weird, wrong, or bad? I started to think of all the misunderstandings and pain I caused others by thinking in black-and-white terms. Sometimes I would believe those who lived differently were strange, and perhaps treated them poorly because of it. Sometimes I would feel attacked or threatened when I was the one being judged as different. I began to see how rigid black-and-white thinking can cause pain to our self and others.

With these thoughts swirling in my head, Don Theo started the ceremony, which included setting our intention or our goals for the day. I set the intention to receive peace, serenity, health, and purpose. One by one we were given a cup of medicinal San Pedro tea, which had a bitter, barky taste, quickly followed by a larger cup of mint tea chaser. Immediately I felt the warm San Pedro liquid enter my digestion system. Filled with San Pedro, we were all loaded onto a waiting bus. An hour bus ride culminated into a zigzag path to the upper point between two mountain peaks. After seeing nothing but the barren, dusty mountain ranges, the first glimpse of Tipón, the Temple of Water, was like an oasis. As we exited the bus, the faint gurgling sound of a tiny creek welcomed us. Steps led us into a giant football field–sized yard. It looked uncommonly manicured and green compared to what we had seen elsewhere. The yard was U-shaped and around three sides were three brick-separated terraces expanding into more and more terraces farther back into the mountains. All along the right side was a channel of water starting high in the mountains, then flowing through Tipón, and continuing its journey past where I first saw it by the bus. The sounds of water were everywhere. It seemed like every sound of water was present: gurgling, churning, splashing, rushing, tinkling, gently falling, and crashing. Each nuance of sound was prominent and meaningful. Being surrounded by the orchestra of water was exhilarating and intoxicating. We stopped at a small covered area with benches. Don Theo spoke of how two civilizations prior to the Incas had built Tipón all without the concrete and metal tools of the later conquering Spaniards. An expert in archeology and anthropology, Don Theo questioned how other anthropologists classify the advancements of civilizations by their advent of pottery. The pre-Inca civilizations created Tipón to harness glacial streams centuries before they ever had pottery. He continued to talk, but I missed what he said because the plant medicine had begun to take effect.

I felt queasy and lightheaded. My ears seemed plugged and open at the same time. During the ceremony I had set an intention for peace, serenity, health, and purpose. The experience of the plant gave me the feeling of peace and serenity. I was very relaxed and didn't want to speak. I felt my voice would break the quiet, calm stillness now engulfing me. As a stressed-out workaholic, I never experienced peace like this before. As we walked, we passed by one area where the water was beneath us, poking through some beautiful stones. I stopped and marveled at its beauty. It seemed to be alive. It was the most beautiful thing I had ever seen, even though it was barely five inches of gently moving water. The sun glistened off each wave and crest. The water seemed to dance as it glided past me. I didn't want to continue walking. I could have stayed in this one spot for the rest of my life. It was pure joy, peace, beauty, and love. The Saint Peter cactus held true to its name and opened the gates of heaven to me here on earth. Pepe saw I had stopped walking, and came over to check on me. I tried to find the words in Spanish, and in English, to tell him what I was experiencing. All I could come up with was "mi corazon," my heart. Pepe replied with a knowing smile, "Yes, your heart is expanding." But it was so much more. I felt my heart was the stream, was the terrace, was the blue sky, was everything all at the same time. I was connected to all. *I was all.*

At the top of the first ledge, the stream from the mountains separated into three lines, then five, then two, and finally came back again to one. I thought of how much my husband, who lived for weekends on our boat, would have enjoyed Tipón. A cloud of sadness descended. I went into a pity party. I was experiencing this alone. Sob, sob, poor me, I am all alone. As soon as the thought entered my mind, the tears came rushing to my eyes. Once again I was abandoned, alone, detached, unloved. Out of nowhere I heard my voice boldly, confidently, authoritatively saying, "No. I am not alone." At least I think it was my voice, and I think it was aloud, but no one else seemed to notice, so I am not sure. I had expected San Pedro to be what I imagine acid to be like. I expected an experience where plants would grow lips and talk to me, but instead it felt like my heart was talking to me, and telling me the wisdom of how we are all connected. I am part of each of those rushing streams. I am part of those puffy clouds. I am part of those magnificent mountains. I am part of every body of water. I am not alone in this moment, and I will never be alone as long as I can remember I am connected to nature. I am one with and part of the all. We can debate whether I had a truly otherworldly connection with nature, or whether the plant medicine shut down my left brain, releasing the feeling of right brain connectedness. You choose. I am just sharing what I experienced because it was the first time I truly felt peace, serenity, connectedness, and unconditional acceptance.

Later in the afternoon after San Pedro's effect faded, we stopped at a restaurant for lunch. The outside of the building looked similar to Poqen Kanchay with its dirty, unkempt concrete walls. Again I prepared myself to be open to the modest offerings of this non-commercialized country. Again I was wrong. As we entered the gates, we saw two magnificent fountains. The suspended entryway bridge into the restaurant would have been welcoming and seemed ostentatious to even the biggest Hollywood star. Our group of fifteen or so sat at a large, long, beautiful dark wood table as staff came from everywhere to take our orders, and ensure we were comfortable. After being fooled again by outside appearances, I began to think about the people by the river the first day. Was my perception wrong? Should I have assumed because they appeared not to have a lot of money they should be pitied? Or is there something for which they should pity *me*? Back in the States we spend lots of money to make our outsides, our homes, our clothes, our bodies look perfect. We shine, color, and dress up everything others might physically see about us in the hopes we will receive acceptance, love, and connection. But here, the outsides didn't seem to matter. Really, what is so important about the outside of the buildings that are only going to be beaten up by the harsh dust of the Peruvian winters? Instead, Peruvians focus on what matters. They focus on making their insides, their truth, their relationships sparkle and shine. They do not do it to impress, but they do it because it brings them joy. The longer I stayed in Peru, the more I found Peruvians are some of the happiest people in the world. They are friendly, smiling, and always celebrating. Americans have fleeting happiness based on transient things like a new purchase, a specific event, or an accomplishment. Peruvians appeared joyful finding bliss in the ordinary and every day. Where Americans are "doing" life, Peruvians are living it.

Before I had left for Peru, my husband and I saw *The Simpsons Movie* at a drive-in theater. Once again Homer Simpson gets himself in trouble and has to try to cross the Alaskan wilderness to catch up with his family. Passed out from exhaustion, an Inuit woman saves him, and nurses him back to health. This healer woman tells him he must have an epiphany, or he will spend the rest of his life alone. She and Homer make the guttural sounds of an Inuit throat song to send him into a vision. Through a vision filled with totem poles and trees that smack him, Homer receives his epiphany. He must save the town of Springfield. With this cartoonish image in my head, I prepared for my first experience with Ayahuasca cactus, also called the vine of death.

After a light dinner, I was told to bundle up because the room was cold, and this plant medicine makes one colder. The ceremony starts late in the evening. Being on Ayahuasca makes one sensitive to light, so it is best taken at night. The ceremony was to focus on cleansing. I thought of everything I wanted to release: taking care of others before myself, being both critical and feeling like a victim, and of course, my poor health. I wanted to release all of the thoughts, beliefs, and unconscious actions I know are harmful to me and to others, but which I just couldn't seem to shake through all those years of therapy. I wanted to let go of the ghosts of all the hurtful, harmful, embarrassing things I have said and done in my life. I wanted a clean, clear slate from which to live.

Armed with a jacket, hat, and gloves, I joined the others in a room where all the windows were blocked by heavy blankets, and one single candle dimly lit the room. Taking Ayahuasca is similar to San Pedro, but the taste is even more bitter and you get no chaser, although I did laugh when they offered a TicTac breath mint to help take away the nasty aftertaste. As I felt the herb enter my body, I became queasy, feeling like at any moment the entire room was going to start spinning. Even though only one candle burned, I could now easily see the faces of the other travelers twenty feet away from me on the other side of the room. Hallucinations started once the medicinal cactus kicked in. Trying to stop the images seemed to make the queasiness increase, so I tried to go with the flow, which was a new concept to me. It appeared the whole room was filled with water. It wasn't a scary "I'm drowning" thing, but more like both watching and being inside a gigantic fish tank. I watched the dolphins and stingray float by, and I tried to rock with the water so I wouldn't get sick.

In each Ayahuasca ceremony, Don Theo would call a few people up one at a time and work with them individually. I was called the first night. Standing in front of the shaman, I was told to say my full name two times. He asked me to walk backwards. I kept walking and walking until I thought I would walk out of the room. I heard Don Theo and Pepe gasp and tell me to stop.

I couldn't make out what they were saying in Spanish, but it sounded like they found the cause of my pain, and it was severe or shocking or difficult to fix. Later, after seeing the individual work of others, I gathered walking backward somehow allowed Don Theo to see our lives and histories. The farther one walked back, the farther back in time the causal trauma was in one's life.

Don Theo approached me and, whispering semi-broken English in my ear, asked if I was married, and how was my marriage. Yes, and good, I responded. He told me I was holding myself back. He asked if I had experienced a trauma or accident when I was younger. I could not recall any childhood trauma, so I said, "I don't know." Pepe assisted Don Theo during the individual work and began waving a condor feather all around my body, trying to remove all of the self-protection and self-restraint. It appeared he was working very hard, and whatever he was trying to remove didn't want to budge.

My individual experience ended with a woman moving her hands from the back of my head down my body to the floor, and having two other people spit citrus cologne, known as Florida Water after the famed Fountain of Youth, at me. After Don Theo and Pepe worked with a few other individuals, music was played. The first song sounded like a funeral march for my old self. The other songs made my head spin, literally, on its own. I felt myself crying, but it was more of a silent scream. This was not your normal Tuesday evening.

The next day I continued to try to remember the childhood incident at the root of my pain, but could not come up with anything. I now felt I had a hairball around my heart, causing my teeth and shoulders to hurt, so I went to Don Theo. The pain I was experiencing was from my inability to release. He and I discussed how I was trying to confine myself into the framework of life I assumed society and family tradition had dictated. I needed to release the life I assumed I had to live. This made sense to me as it aligned with all the work I had completed through counseling. The trouble, however, was not understanding the problem in my head, but in releasing my heart. Don Theo started work on my heart by blowing tobacco smoke and Florida Water at my chest, and he prescribed a special rose-petal tea for me every morning I was in Peru.

The plant, tea, and insight all began to have their effect as I slowly began to chip away at the apparent failures in my life, and redefine what success looked like to me. Interestingly, I did not start imagining a new career, an amount of money, a new home, or some other tangible description. Success began to take the form of being true to myself, having a pure heart, being grateful, finding time to be in nature, being positive, calm, and peaceful, and taking care of my body. I wanted to be a joyful Peruvian, not a stressed-out American.

RELEASE AND RECHARGE

My second experience using San Pedro medicinal cactus was at the beautifully terraced Pisa'q. Pisa'q appeared a hundred times larger than Tipón; in fact, it is eight thousand feet larger than the famous Machu Picchu. It has no water elements like Tipón, only layer after layer of terracing hugging and forming to the contours of the mountains. More tourists were at this site, but due to its size, we had plenty of space to take in the majesty of this amazing blending of nature and man-made construction. We walked up to the top of the terracing and wound our way around the mountain. At one point as we walked around the bend from one side of the mountain to the other, we found a manmade cavern dug into the mountain. Inside it was ten degrees colder, very peaceful and quiet.

On the other side of the mountain, we saw what looked like an ancient city. Many of the building walls still stood, and the bottom remnants of others remained. Among the ruins were a series of five perfectly carved stones arranged in what may have been an ancient chamber. Something drew me to these stones. As I stood within this structure, I began to sway and my breathing became heavy. It was similar to the feeling of being overtaken physically during the first Ayahuasca ceremony. It was such a powerful and uncontrollable experience I became frightened, and ran to Don Theo. "Don Theo, what are those stones? What are they for?" Don Theo replied, "What do you perceive?" I did not speak it, but I perceived nothing. I was in such a habit of asking others what was truth, what was right and wrong, I did not even stop to consider what *I* was feeling. I expected Don Theo to tell me. I started to walk away, dejected.

I had come to Peru to be healed *by* a shaman. If I had the answers, I would have already fixed my health problems. Don Theo saw my frustration and disappointment. "See that fountain?" he said as he gestured toward a small pool with water flowing down on different levels. "Cleanse your heart in the water. Breathe out to release the bad. Picture an open window around your heart." As I drew water to my face, I felt emotion and pressure build in my chest. I used my hands to push this emotion down, not touching my body, but working on a force just outside of my body. I pushed harder and harder, again and again until I felt the pressure decrease and disappear. It was as if I were pushing layers of mud off my body. But this mud was unseen and abstract.

This experience was the first time I felt emotional energy as a part of me. Much is spoken about emotional energy through acupuncture, Reiki, and other energetic modalities. The idea of energy can be very foreign to the Western world, but it is very common to many Asians. The feeling and concept were not familiar to me at the time. It felt like a thing of me and in me, but not necessarily me; rather, it was a force working in the background.

I believe that day I had an energetic release of all the pain and negativity I had held onto over the years. Years of limiting beliefs, regrets, and loss caked up my energy system. This was the "mud" I felt. In order to feel the pure, loving spirit, I needed to remove this muck. Imagine if your garden hose was clogged with dirt. The pure, clean water would not be able to flow easily, and it would either build up pressure, or if some water were released, it would be soiled by the dirt it had to push through to get out. I had lived many years with beautiful, positive, joyous energy backed up, clogging my system. Now this energy just wanted to flow freely. At times during my life, some positive energy would come through, but it was always coated with the mucky debris of jealously, defeat, and sadness. My experience at Pisa'q released my clog and allowed me to begin to feel an incredible power waiting to flow freely. I began to feel liberated, free of my past, unafraid of my future, peaceful, and calm. Like the mineral-water colonic had removed the buildup of food and toxins in my body, my experience at Pisa'q removed the energetic buildup so my energetic-emotional system could work perfectly again, just as it was designed to do.

The theme for the second Ayahuasca ceremony was health. My guess is my health depended on sleep because I slept during most of the ceremony. Don Theo said to try to stay awake, but I couldn't keep my eyes open. The only memorable part of the process was a voice (my voice?) like the one at Tipón saying, "I am done crying for my childhood." I felt I was now done living in the past, being a victim, and keeping myself from moving forward.

Don Theo mentioned working with plant medicine is always different. When you expect a specific outcome, you miss the true experience, saying, "We are working with the power of the plant, not a specific effect." The experience we have is different, depending on our intention. It is about accepting what is there, not expecting or trying to force a specific result.

One of the last sites we visited in Peru was Q'espiwara. This was an ancient ceremonial site, and not a usual tour stop; however, not much of what we did or saw was on the normal Globus Tour. Q'espi means mirror or reflection. Wara is the name of the initiation clothing worn. The site, at the bottom of a valley guarded by tall, ancient trees, was beautiful. I marveled at the now-small and insignificant stream trickling in the chasm left by a powerful river that once cut out the steep, jagged walls. Closer to the start of the basin was a collection of rocks, which were surely the remnants of a waterfall. Across from the rocks was a huge stone with an intricate carving. I am still amazed how the stones were carved so precisely without the use of metal tools.

As I sat on a large rock overlooking the carving, Don Theo said to let the waters wash away our pain. I closed my eyes and slowly my head lowered. My body began to rock and spin as it had during the first Ayahuasca ceremony. I was not being cleansed by the sound of the water, like in Tipón, or the physical feel of the water, like during the start of my release at Pisa'q. This time I felt only the *energy* of the water cleansing my mind, emotions, spirit, and body. Like the feeling of joy at Tipón, and release in Pisa'q, Q'espiwara now filled me with power and perfect health. When I rose from the rock, I felt at least ten years younger. I had no muscle pain or sloped shoulders from aging. My usual stomach ailments with were gone. My footsteps were easy and seemingly effortless. My mind was clear. My energy was high. I think I could have flown back up the mountain if I tried. I was recharged, and I had finally shed the anger, fear, doubt, pain, anxiety, and disappointment I had been carrying with me for years. My physical pain was not due solely to my biology—It was due to all the emotional pain I had brought on by restraining myself in the stress of a black-and-white world.

The theme of the final Ayahuasca ceremony was vision. We gathered in the same chamber as the other Ayahuasca ceremonies, but the tea tasted stronger, and we started later at night so I assumed the dose was larger than the other times. I was invigorated and awake, but for the first hour or so, I did not feel anything except a little nausea. Two people were physically ill this time, causing some serious retching. I was afraid it would be contagious. As I relaxed and focused on anything I could, instead of hearing the heaving, I received a vision. I saw carved tribal drawings. When I saw feathers and shells on leather, I realized it was some sort of necklace being placed around my head. It was an initiation ceremony, welcoming me into a life of healing. But as with the other nights, that was it. No extensive mystical journey for me. My body shut down, and I was asleep, waking occasionally to see dark shadows in the room that looked like elders overseeing the ceremony.

I knew nothing about the Peruvian beliefs before going on this journey. Although Peru was life changing for me, I did not convert to or currently practice the pre-Inca culture and Peruvian shamanism belief systems. The experience was more about my healing than any religion. I have a respect for the shamanistic practices, but I have not become like the other travelers on my journey who brought out their altars on the first day.

It is also important to note that although the medicinal cactus released me from my energetic pain, there were other factors in my healing. The food cleanse the month before became an eye-opener to how various foods were affecting my body. I walked ten miles every day before leaving for Peru in order to be prepared for the altitude and hiking we would do. This brought my body into the best shape it had been in years. I consciously journaled every day and processed the wisdom shared by Don Theo. Together, working on my mind, body, and spirit, I received the healing I desired. More importantly I began to realize how each of these areas affected how I felt, and how what I did or didn't do contributed to my mental and physical health.

My adventure in healing gave me the ultimate sendoff to show me all I had learned. August fifteenth was the final day of the official trip, and most of the participants, including our American tour guides, left to return home. Pepe escorted the five who stayed to Machu Picchu. Here is where I started to experience a new way of living: living fully, living boldly, and truly *living* my life.

I first noticed my new sense of joy and peace on the bus ride up to Machu Picchu. It is a pretty dangerous trek. Extra-large buses take groups of tourists up to the site by traversing narrow dirt roads, seemingly only one car length wide. As the "road" curved to rise up the next incline, sometimes the bus had to maneuver a three-point turn to make it around a tight hairpin curve. To add to the insanity, as our bus was going up, other buses were coming down, trying to share this tiny dirt road smashed between a mountain and a thousand-foot drop-off. The old Melissa would have been panicking, terrified through the entire ordeal, knowing we were moments away from plummeting to our death. My entire body would have been tense, assuming I had some control over how the bus driver drove, or what our fate would be. Instead, I looked out the window, enjoying the spectacular view, trusting it would not be the last thing I would see. And if this was to be my last day on earth, I was fine with that, too. I began to experience the feeling of peaceful Accepting joy.

We did make it to the top and began to explore the amazing city built long before the Inca civilization. At one point, we were guided gingerly by Pepe to descend what appeared to be a six-inch-wide rock staircase down to another level of Machu Picchu. Like the bus ride up, we had no guardrails or safety features. There was just the rock wall to the right, small slippery stones to walk down, and an incredible drop-off into the valley below. A sweet woman from our group was terrified to step down, and although I was also concerned, instead I took her hand and comforted her as we made our way safely down the precarious stairs. Again, I felt a sense of peace, support, and comfort. And this time I also felt compassion for my fellow traveler. I lovingly guided her through the peace and support I felt internally. Having descended, she was overcome with the strength and power she now recognized in herself. I witnessed her triumph over fear, and it was amazing. By being empowered myself, I can help others to realize their own power.

Unbeknownst to us, during our return from Machu Picchu to Poqen Kanchay, an eight-point earthquake was occurring in Lima. As we were in motion and quite far from the epicenter, we did not notice the ground shake. And none of the staff told us of the earthquake. Through their compassionate nurturing, they wanted us to have a good night's sleep, without an ounce of worry. The next morning we finally heard the news. The other travelers were worried. What state was the city of Lima in? Was our flight out of Lima still scheduled? What would happen to us? In contrast, I was still in a place of centered peace. I calmly instructed the others to check on flights at the local Internet café, and alleviated their worries, explaining we could always stay a few more days at Poqen Kanchay. I had no worry, no fear, or no stressed-out thinking we were going to die because of this situation. I was embracing a new peaceful, accepting attitude.

We made our flights with no incident and safely flew to Miami in the evening, but I could not sleep. All I could do was peacefully gaze into the bright nighttime stars, so close to my airplane window I thought I could touch them. Unfortunately, I was soon to learn how easily I could lose the peace of Peru.

BACK TO REALITY

When my plane landed in Miami, I was immediately overcome with the frantic nature of our Western culture, and I unconsciously jumped into the fray. I was overcome with worry I would miss my transfer. My stress level increased as I calculated the best customs line to choose, and the most efficient paths to take through the airport. My anxiety increased even though everything I was doing ensured I would most definitely catch my flight. Then I began to feel twinges of pain—pain I had not felt in days now coursed through my belly and my shoulders. The stress of making my flight, going through customs, and entering back into the land of Starbucks and deadlines made my stomach flip. It was a slap-in-the-face realization.

Here was a prime example of what caused me so much pain in my day-to-day life. All the beautiful pain-free lightness in my body began to be covered in the soot of stress. It may have taken two shamans, five plant-induced magical journeys, and ten days of being cared for unconditionally to remove all of the pain in my body, but I am more powerful than all that. I was able to make the pain return all by myself, and in less than ten minutes.

As I traveled from Miami to the Chicago airport to my house, I felt more and more of the joyful peace of Peru disappear as my body became tight and unsettled. Returning to my day-to-day life, it became so very clear how I lived in a state of constant worry, hustle, anxiety, and drive. Not only were there stressors from daily life, but I also added even more through my own mental anxiety. We Type A's are so good at focusing on the future, and worrying about the past, we do not live in the moment. We are always on the go, feeling we are being left behind. Or we are stuck in the past complaining about what should have happened, focusing on the perceived pain and injustice in our lives. We are focused so much on what is outside, we have lost sight of the joy inside.

The evening I returned home, my husband really wanted to go with a group of friends to see a local music band. After all I had been through, I simply wanted a quiet evening, but after ten days away from my husband, I went along. Surreal does not begin to explain the situation. Our group of twenty people bumped and pushed their way to the event, but I seemed to float behind them, amazed at the chaos they were creating. As we tried to enter, the doorman grabbed my wrist tightly. "You don't have enough tickets. She can't go in." From my state of calm, I could feel the angry vibrations from this man. Normally I would have internalized the pain of his anger, and also added on fear of what would happen if they didn't allow me in. I would have taken the incident personally, and used it to fuel an attack on myself and my right to exist. Instead, I felt as if I was standing still, and the entire world was moving around me. I felt as if I was watching from someplace else. After finally being let in, I found a quiet place to recollect myself. It was then I realized there was a different way to live, and I was on the right path to change my life. It meant changing not the outsides of my life—my job, my friends, or my hobbies—but changing the inside of my life. I wanted to feel like I did in Peru, and I wanted to feel the same way every minute of every day, no matter where I was, or who was around me. But how could I do so when the society I lived in did not reflect the same pace and focus on life? I thought about going back to Peru on a regular basis to receive the expert care of the shamans, but the idea didn't seem practical. Besides, what good was it to go to Peru if I could undo any healing in a matter of moments? I needed to create ways to have the same Peruvian feeling during my daily life. The Type-Me Habits began to take form.

UNCOVERING THE TYPE-ME HABITS

My Peruvian experience provided me with the firsthand knowledge—I could be peaceful, serene, happy, and amazingly healthy. I had felt it the day at Q'espiwara, and I didn't ever want to feel old, pained, stressed, and generally yucky again. The plant medicine had allowed me a glimpse of how life could be, and I knew I could get that way again without the use of medicinal cactus. My quest now was trying to obtain and maintain a healthy status now that I was back home. While in Peru, I was away from the hustle and bustle of my average day filled with traffic, deadlines, and difficult people. I was able to be in a blissful, calm state. How could I now integrate what I learned in Peru into my everyday life? How could I keep from locking up my heart again? How could I keep the icky energetic mud from accumulating? I wanted to uncover how I could remain mentally, emotionally, and physically healthy every day, and in every situation. This search for answers not only led me to define and incorporate the Type-Me Habits into my own life, but also awakened a desire to help others do the same.

As I began to embrace my Type Me, I felt the desire to become a psychologist re-emerge (I first had it in high school), as did the idea of becoming a life coach, a career becoming more mainstream. I decided to hire a coach to help me uncover what my new career should be, and so I could also experience firsthand what it was like to work with a coach to see if it was what I was meant to do.

Through working with a coach, I came to recognize helping

others was the right career path for me. As I began coach training, I realized my training would not only be in the classroom, but in my everyday life as well. My father had just been diagnosed with terminal cancer. This dire situation gave me the chance to practice the new process I developed to help me find peace. I learned to be actively Aware of my emotions and reactions to the downturns and challenges of his health, instead of being a victim of them. I learned how Accepting the truth of the situation provided me with peace, and generated Alternatives in the way I acted, reacted, and experienced his journey and my grief. And finally I learned Acting on my Daily Habits gave me a firm emotional and psychological base.

Between dealing with my father's cancer, training to become a certified coach, my continued search for resources and tools to bring my Peru experience to the States, and beginning to work with coaching clients, the Type-Me Habits were revealed and developed. Using Awareness, Acceptance, Alternatives, and Action personally, and with my clients, I learned how to have power in every situation, how to be unaffected by external circumstances, and how to find a sea of stress-free solutions. I learned how to create a less stressful state of mind. I began to craft my personal Daily Habits that keep me continuously living joyfully and peacefully, no matter what is happening in my life. Using the Type-Me process helped me through a job change and subsequent layoff, as well as through the stresses of starting my own business. The practices helped me find peace and joy even through the ups and downs of my father's illness and death. I learned how the stress, worry, and physical pain returned when I stopped my practices. And I learned how I could change the bleakness of anything happening to me by truly embracing these habits.

Now I practice the Type-Me Habits of Awareness, Acceptance, Alternatives, and Action daily, and I have so much joy and pride when people tell me they admire my peaceful aura. How I currently experience my daily life is so far away from the stress, fear, depression, sadness, and ill health that used to surround me. A dear friend who knew me at the height of my illness and stress is especially aware of and in awe of the changes to my attitude, personality, and joy of life. I am thrilled to have uncovered the Type-Me Habits, and to be able to teach them to others so they too can enjoy the amazingly calm, beautiful life this world has to offer.

1 McLeod, S. A. (2011). Type A Personality. Retrieved from http://www.simplypsychology.org/personality-a.html

2 Money, Dava M. Ed. Director of Creative Healing Institute, Fairfax VA, https://www.youtube.com/watch?v=8fNPyAUcap8

3 Tolle, Eckhart, *The Power of Now – A Guide to Spiritual Enlightenment*, New World Library, 1999.

4 Beck, Martha, *The Joy Diet – 10 Daily Practices for a Happier Life*, Crown Publishers, 2003.

5 Mitchell, Stephen, *Tao Te Ching – A New English Version*, Harper Perennial, 1988.

6 Ruiz, Don Miguel, *The Voice of Knowledge – A Practical Guide to Inner Peace*, Amber-Allen Publishing, 2004.

7 Bolte Taylor, Dr. Jill, *My Stroke of Insight: A Brain Scientist's Personal Journey*, Penguin, 2006, pages 20–21.

8 Huffington, Arianna, *Thrive: The Third Metric to Redefining Success and Creating a Life of Well-Being, Wisdom, and Wonder*, Harmony Books, 2014, page 15.

9 Rensink, Ronald A., *When Good Observers Go Bad: Change Blindness, Inattentional Blindness, and Visual Experience*, Cambridge Basic Research, 2000.

10 Bolte Taylor, Dr. Jill, *The Neuroanatomical Transformation of the Teenage Brain*, TEDx Youth, https://www.youtube.com/watch?v=PzT_SBl31-s

11 Phrase "dirty pain" attributed to Stephen Hayes.

12 Bolte Taylor, Dr. Jill, *My Stroke of Insight: A Brain Scientist's Personal Journey*, Penguin, 2006, page 13.

13 Larsen, Stephen, *The Fundamentalist Mind: How Polarized Thinking Imperils Us All*, The Theosophical Publishing House, 2007, pg. 62.

14 *The Empowerment Show*, http://www.itsmylifeinc.com/2013/12/hard-wiring-happiness-with-dr-rick-hanson-on-the-empowerment-show/

15 Hanson, Dr. Rick Ph.D., *Buddha's Brain: The Practical Neuroscience of Happiness, Love & Wisdom*, New Harbinger Publications, Inc., 2009, page 100.

BOOKS

Allison, Jay and Gediman, Dan editors, *This I Believe: The Personal Philosophies of Remarkable Men and Women*, Holt Paperbacks 2006

Beck, Martha, *Finding Your Own North Star: Claiming the Life You Were Meant to Live*, Three Rivers Press, New York, 2001

Beck, Martha, *Finding Your Way in a Wild New World: Reclaim Your True Nature to Create the Life You Want*, Free Press, 2012

Beck, Martha, *Steering by Starlight: Finding Your Right Life No Matter What!* Rodale Inc. 2008

Bolte Taylor, Jill Ph.D., *My Stroke of Insight: A Brain Scientist's Personal Journey*, Viking Penguin 2006

Hanson, Dr. Richard Ph.D., with Mendius, Richard M.D., *Buddha's Brain: The Practical Neuroscience of Happiness, Love & Wisdom*, New Harbinger Publications, Inc. 2009

Hay, Louise L., *You Can Heal Your Life*, Hay House, Inc. 1987

Hayes, Steven C. Ph.D. with Smith, Spencer, *Get Out of Your Mind & Into Your Life: The New Acceptance & Commitment Therapy*, New Harbinger Publications, Inc. 2005

Katie, Byron with Mitchell, Stephen, *Loving What Is: Four Questions That Can Change Your Life*, Three Rivers Press 2002

Larsen, Stephen, *The Fundamentalist Mind: How Polarized Thinking Imperils Us All*, The Theosophical Publishing House 2007

Newberg, Andrew M.D., and Waldman, Mark Robert, *How God Changes Your Brain: Breakthrough Findings From a Leading Neuroscientist*, Ballatine Books 2009

Ruiz, Don Miguel, *The Four Agreements: A Practical Guide to Personal Freedom*, Amber-Allen Publishing 1997

Ruiz, Don Miguel, *The Voice of Knowledge: A Practical Guide to Inner Peace*, Allen-Amber Publishing Inc., 2004

Tolle, Eckhart, *The Power of Now: A Guide to Spiritual Enlightenment*, New World Library 1999

VIDEO

Dispenza, Dr. Joe, "Your Immortal Brain: Mastering the Art of Observation," 2005

STUDIES

Costafreda SG, Brammer MJ, David AS, Fu CH, "Predictors of amygdala activation during the processing of emotional stimuli: a meta-analysis of 385 PET and fMRI studies," Institute of Psychiatry, King's College London, UK. s.costafreda@iop.kcl.ac.uk, Brain Res Rev. June 2008, http://www.ncbi.nlm.nih.gov/pubmed/18076995

Hölzelab, Britta K., Carmodyc, James, Vangela, Mark, Congletona, Christina, Yerramsettia, Sita M., Gardab, Tim, Lazara, Sara W., "Mindfulness practice leads to increases in regional brain gray matter density," Psychiatry Research Neuroimaging, Volume 191, Issue 1, 30 January 2011, http://www.psyn-journal.com/article/S0925-4927%2810%2900288-X/abstract

Lutz A., Brefczynski-Lewis J., Johnstone T. Davidson R.J., "Regulation of the neural circuitry of emotion by compassion meditation: effects of meditative expertise," University of Wisconsin, Madison, Wisconsin, United States, 26 March 2008, http://www.ncbi.nlm.nih.gov/pubmed/18365029

ARTICLES

Bhanoo, Sindya N., "How Meditation May Change the Brain," New York Times, 28 January 2011 http://well.blogs.nytimes.com/2011/01/28/how-meditation-may-change-the-brain/

McLeod, S. A. (2011). "Type A Personality," Retrieved from http://www.simplypsychology.org/personality-a.html

ACKNOWLEDGMENTS

I am eternally grateful to my husband, who has been a constant support and loving partner throughout the ups and downs of my transition from Type A to Type Me. Thank you for seeing the diamond in the rough and sticking with me through all these years.

Special thanks to all of my clients who, knowingly and unknowingly, helped me formulate the concepts and examples shared in this book.

Thank you to Tamera Harrison, Sam Hull, Roni Weiner Pressler, and Renee Renz for sharing their personal Type-Me stories.

I am grateful to:

• Susan Barker, Amanda Both, Bailey Both, Fred Broviak, Maria Caruso, Jim and Martha Curnow, Joe Diamond, Katie Krizka, Anthony Losacco, Valerie Mikes, Diane Testa, and Kieta Wheeler for providing input during the many revisions;

• Melinda Camardella and Meredith Colby for sharing their experiences of working with me;

• Ann Potts for getting the fire back in my belly when I hit a wall;

• Erin Brown for helping me to focus my first full manuscript;

• Jen Duchene, Donna Scott-Nusrala, and Nancy Lee Segal for getting me out of my own way so I could see the truth of what I am here to share;

• Grant Polachek for his help in wordsmithing the Type A experience;

• Alex Hoffman and the Arlington Heights Memorial Library for their help with my video; and

• Amy Quale, Connie Anderson, Wise Ink Creative Publishing, and Pubslush for making this book a reality.

A big thank you to all those who participated in the crowdfunding campaign that made this book a reality: Melissa Amling, Nancy Bach, Erin Bernau, Tami Blackmore, Sue Bock, Linda Both, Julie Brennan Reidy, Paige Brooks, Tempia Courts, Amanda Cozzo, Martha Curnow, Meira Eliot, Beatrice Figueroa, Edie Heisler, The Todd Heisler Family,

Linda Hickok, Anthony Hidoo, Roger Hinze, Ginger Kadlec, Christina Lassota, Joshua Little, Judy Maritato, Jill May, Matt McClain, Sharo Moceri, Virginia Morin, Anatoliy Pak, Amy Quale, Michele Reining Malo, Diana Schneidman, Rachel Schreer, Sheryl Shields, Jennifer Stacy, Diane Testa, Alissia Thompson, Cindy Trawinski, and Kieta Wheeler.

Also, thanks to all those who helped with and attended fundraisers: Sarah Karnes, Jill May, Danielle McLaughlin, Mihaela Marcusanu, Kieta Wheeler, Body-Education, The Gathering Lighthouse, and Regus USA.

MELISSA HEISLER is a recovering Type A. After ten years managing and directing theatrical productions and seventeen years in corporate marketing, the stress of high-pressure, deadline-driven jobs led to her own ill health, mentally and physically. This started her search for a long-lasting means of approaching each situation with ease, contentment, and power. She developed her system for managing stress and has been leading a more peaceful life ever since. In her coaching, Melissa uses this system again and again to guide professionals to live better. She has a master's degree in integrated marketing communication.

Made in the USA
Monee, IL
09 June 2023

35208276R00132